On The Outside Looking In

by

Joseph Wheeler

Introduction

On The Outside Looking In is about how I came to view the American Experiment through my own experiences and that of black people around me. It is not a complaint, although there is some of that in this book. It is more of an observation of life, or an assessment of life, following the Civil Rights Movement of the 1950s and 1960s. It's about history, combined with my personal stories to help the reader follow me on my journey to becoming a preacher and a civil rights activist. I have tried to be brutally transparent, so the reader should expect a few racy episodes. I guess I could be described as a heathen with few guardrails when I was a teen. But you won't find any immoral acts that do not occur in the Bible.

Through my stories, I hope to reveal some of the shortcomings of African American culture along with the beauty of it. The reader may be challenged to look at some of the strengths of the black protestant church and some weaknesses. I talk about faith in a living God. I invite the reader to consider the white backlash to any advancement by African Americans or any perceived advancement. Critics may say this is a book about victimization. I beg to differ. Usually, the ones who use this label of "victimization" are those who benefit well from the system. They either do not know the history of African Americans, or they choose to operate in ignorance. Chained in the bottom of slave ships, millions of Africans were brought to the West as victims of the slave trade. A civil war ended the legal institution of slavery, but it did not change the hearts of the enslavers nor their descendants. Successive generations of white lawmakers continue to devise new schemes to undermine the progress of the descendants of the slaves.

Dr. Martin Luther King Jr. said it best when he said, "He that gets behind in a race must forever stay behind or run faster than the man ahead of him." I might add, "That is our dilemma." If the managers and referees of the tournament are engaging in rigging the game, the outcome is predictable. We must demand that the game be conducted according to fair rules. We are not victims if the rules are fair. Too often in America, the rules keep changing as progress is made by African Americans and other marginalized groups. I try to point out systemic racism in the daily struggle of black folks, but I am fully aware of the great achievements of black people in modern times despite the opposition. The greatness of black people swells up from antiquity. Those with power have controlled the false narratives about history. They ban history books and Advanced Placement (AP) courses in Black studies. They attack Critical Race Theory (CRT) out of fear that all American students may understand structural racism and work to dismantle it. These "system managers" would rather point to the crumbs they allow to fall from the table to help a few, while putting policies in place that foster ignorance, poverty, and crime for the masses.

The economic needs of the "landowners" caused Whites to deal with Black folks deceitfully since the arrival of the kidnapped Africans. To this day, deceitful rhetoric and policies continue to impede the progress of African Americans. After the Reconstruction Era, Whites used the Black Codes to regulate the freedom of Black folks. These were unjust laws with fines, so that Black folks could be arrested for loitering and hired out to a plantation owner to work off the fines. Not long after the Black Codes were established, Jim Crow laws were put in place. Separate but equal facilities dotted the South, but they were anything but equal. During the early 1900s, leading into the 1950s and 60s, intimidation was used against Black leaders, churches, and groups. Thriving black communities like Greenwood, a black enclave of Tulsa, Oklahoma in 1921, and Rosewood, Florida in 1923 were burned to the ground to contain black energy. When the Civil Rights Movement came on the scene, blacks were spied on by the FBI, and names of prominent black leaders were placed on the FBI watch list. They were tagged as communists, socialists, or some other kind of radicals. Even though their claims were just, who were they to complain about it?

Members of the White power structure are the custodians of the American Experiment. They administer the United States Constitution. They decided who should enjoy the American dream. They even have black sympathizers. The Homestead Act of 1862 was meant to benefit whites as they settled in the West. 160 acres went to the adult head of the household. Most of the recipients of these government benefits were European peasants. The GI Bill of 1944 was meant to benefit Whites as well, so when we consider "white privilege," the history of it is well established. Many black military personnel received less than honorable discharges, which made them susceptible to discrimination when it came to the GI Bill. Systemic racism was baked into the making of the U.S. military since its inception. Even the Welfare programs penalized black families in that adult males were suspects in the homes. In this book, I discuss job discrimination, discrimination in promotions, and training; based on my own personal experiences while working with the Clayton County, Georgia NAACP.

Finally, On the Outside Looking In, does not suggest we stay this way. I hope to illustrate how the white power structure fights against attempts by black people to advance in this society by using political policies, name calling, using other blacks who benefit from the system; co-opting movements; buying off civil rights leaders by giving them inside jobs and flushing civil rights organizations with money; and allowing the corruption within to destroy them.

By knowing the tactics of our opponents, we should be better prepared to develop strategies for progress. We must undergo a transformation. We must renew our minds through study and grappling with our inner selves. For me, the Bible is a great source for self-examination. Many of the habits I took on as a child hindered my own progress. I had low self-esteem because I internalized many of the negative things told to me by society and other broken people in my community. I owe apologies to many people for passing on my brokenness. When we learn better, we should do better, and that's what I have been trying to do. I know that learning is a lifelong process and so is spiritual growth.

Because our skin color has been made a stigma, we owe it to ourselves, our sisters and brothers on the continent of Africa, in South America, the Islands, and in Europe to work together to find common solutions to our problems. We must work to dispel suspicion among members of our race and learn about our shared oppression as we build a brighter tomorrow.

Then we will not be on the outside looking in, because we will have created a more favorable system.

Dedication

I want to dedicate this book to my late mother, Glendora Miller. She had many dreams and aspirations, but the society she grew up in didn't nourish them. Not once did I hear her complain. Like so many others around her, she learned to make do with what she had. Her kindness and love for people were passed on to her children. She taught us to value education and hard work. Mother was a gentle, powerful force, and my first teacher.

Acknowledgements

I have so many people to thank for inspiring me to write this book. First, I want to thank Valness Wheeler, aka, Vanessa who labored with me to get our family out of the Sutton Homes Projects of San Antonio, Texas. She gave birth to our beautiful daughter Aundria Latrice Wheeler, who became my driving force against poverty and an unjust system. I thank my first-grade teacher Mrs. Florine Buchanan and all those black educators of West Helena, Arkansas who instilled in me a sense of pride and determination. I'm grateful to all the men and women I served with in the U.S. Army who contributed to my educational development. To my professors at Beulah Heights University for giving me a chance to grow and teach there. Thank you to the dynamic faculty at the Interdenominational Theological Center for helping me to adjust my religious lenses by challenging my wrong assumptions about my faith. I want to thank my grandchildren Carleesiya Miller, Carlos D. Miller, and Queen N. Miller along with my two great granddaughters Noemi and Kaydence McClain.

About the author

Joseph Wheeler served as a Military Policeman in the U.S. Army for seven years and three months. He served thirteen months in Wackernheim a suburb of Mainz, Germany from 1981 to 1982. His mission there was to safeguard nuclear missiles. He served in Livorno, Italy from 1984-87. In Italy he and others founded the Gospel Fellowship Church where he pastored for 3 years. After earning his high school diploma from the Big Bend Community College of Washington state, he attended the University of Maryland that had a satellite campus in Italy.

Wheeler earned his B.A. degree in Biblical Studies at Beulah Heights Bible College (now Beulah Heights University) in Atlanta in 1994. He was serving as an associate minister at the New Macedonia Baptist Church in Riverdale, Georgia, where he was ordained in the Baptist faith under Pastor Gerry T. Anderson. He went on to serve as assistant pastor at Double Springs Baptist Church in Conyers, Georgia during his studies at Beulah Heights. He has graced the pulpits of many churches throughout the Metro-Atlanta area.

After earning his Master of Divinity Degree in 2000 at the Interdenominational Theological Center (ITC) in Atlanta, Wheeler went back to Beaulah Heights University to teach for a few years. He was elected president of the Clayton County, Georgia branch of the NAACP in 1993 and served until 2002. He, along with other NAACP members, engaged in many local civil rights battles. He helped to form other civic groups to solve local problems. Wheeler asked Elijah Summit Mason leaders to join him to start the Martin Luther King Jr parade in Clayton County around 1996. The parade still happens each year. Today, he is still a civil rights activist with the National Action Network, a civil rights group founded by the Rev. Al Sharpton. Wheeler works with and advises many black community leaders in the state of Georgia and other states.

Our struggle with the American experiment is not over

I invite you to come with me as I share my story. I do not boast about being an authority on civil rights, especially after talking to more seasoned veterans of the movement. Yet, we all have a journey and mine led me to get involved with the NAACP and serve in the capacity of branch president. I have tried to be very transparent about the way I appropriated my NAACP training to do the work in the field. I gained knowledge as I did the work. I carried deep concerns about the black community during my last two years of service in the U.S. Army. These concerns bubbled over in 1987 when I returned to the United States. In telling my story, I hope to inspire others to get involved in their community and work to improve it. I hope to encourage the men and women of Clayton County and elsewhere who worked for change to know that your work is not in vain. I feel this book is necessary because we don't want the story of the civil rights leaders in Clayton County to be forgotten. This book can also serve as a reminder to young people that earnest sacrifice can bring progress.

It is also my hope that this book will remind all of us that the struggle is not over. I never thought I would see a black President of the United States in my lifetime. But Mr. Obama's presidency highlighted the deep-seated racism that had been simmering underneath. The election of Mr. Donald J. Trump was a mighty statement sent by white nationalists to

Americans of color. On August 4, 2021, Fox News anchorman, Tucker Carlson flew to Hungary to broadcast and showcase some of the good things about that fascist government. The Trump backlash following his defeat in 2020 led to the January 6th, 2021, insurrection. Supporters of the Make America Great Again (MAGA) movement sought to downplay this great threat to U.S. democracy. Commentator Don Calloway said it best when he points out that this is a reaction to the rising tide of an educated, multiracial, citizenry vying for more economic, political, and social inclusion into the American experiment. We are no longer satisfied with living on the fringes of this republic. No longer are we just pleading for an end to structural racism, we are demanding it.

The mainstream media have been complicit in hiding the true intentions of the racist element in this country. During the Trump years, Steve Bannon, Stephen Miller, along with other sympathizers have been trying to do their part to hold back the full inclusion of people of color. Trump told the American people not to worry about Covid-19, and that it would disappear miraculously. Even as he was spreading this false information, thousands of U.S. citizens were dying, many of whom were disproportionately black and brown people. Republicans have been attacking the Affordable Care Act (ACA), or as the racists call it, Obamacare, because they want to deny healthcare to the most vulnerable, who are black, brown, and poor White citizens. In the April 9, 1990, Vol. 135, No. 15

issue of TIME Magazine the question was asked, "What will the United States be like when Whites are no longer the majority?" This is a question we should all be pondering, and not just in our universities but in our communities as well, at our churches, lodges, beauty salons, barber shops, and other gathering places. Black and Brown students must become aggressive in acquiring the skills in those fields where they are under-represented today. We must insist on occupying top spaces in the CIA, FBI, CDC, Pentagon, and every sphere of American life. Today, the question to our children must not simply be "What do you want to be when you grow up?" The question should be "How do you plan to make a difference?" There was a reason why Trump, Reagan, G.W. Bush, and other recent Republicans surrounded themselves with majority White men. These were optics that reinforced the image of White supremacy.

During the August 8, 2018, Charlottesville's alt-right protest, the neo-Nazis were shouting the "The Jews will not replace us." Of course, they were not only singling out Jews. They were also reacting to the changing of America. The recent census shows that the number of White Americans have declined by 8%, while people of color have been making steady increases. This is the reality that the alt-right is responding to, and whether it is voter suppression measures, opposition to Covid-19 mitigation measures, resistance to teaching Critical Race Theory, or blocking gun violence legislation, the aim is still the same, which is to stop the rise and progress of people of color. The media nor the politicians can come out and say this with a straight face. But we must be sophisticated enough to see through the fog of misinformation.

Finally, a dream sown in the soil of truth will find a way to sprout up, no matter how the elements behave. Our ancestors dreamed of a world where their humanity would not be under constant assault. They wanted to return to the glory days when they shared with the world treasures of beauty in terms of civilization, art, and culture. Theirs was and still is a religion of love for humanity, and all of God's creation. Amid this political and spiritual upheaval, we must not lose our way. We must not become disheartened. The star of due North is still shining brightly directing us to freedom, and that star is God himself in my opinion.

I have come to believe in a wise, all-knowing God who shows up in the darkest hour bearing gifts of hope and supernatural powers that surpass the understanding of common men and women. At least this has been my experience along my journey. At times this man-made system called the U.S. government has been hostile to the whole Black race, and I have watched politicians introduce new strategies, accompanied with fresh talking points. It seems the racists pride themselves on being as cunning now as they were during the colonial period with the Indigenous people, or when they went into Asia, Africa, India, and other lands to colonize, enslave, and exploit the people. Today, that spirit is being challenged globally and here at home. The information age is presenting new challenges to oppressors.

Right wing extremists in Germany, Hungary, Italy, and in the Americas are responding sometimes violently. They see the handwriting on the wall. Nuclear bombs are in the hands of too many people now for one country to threaten the others. Modern terrorists have demonstrated the extremes by which they are willing to go to make their points, so violence is not the answer. We must be willing to share this space on earth respectfully with each other. Republican policies tend to ration out the American dream in small portions to marginalized groups of Americans. They hope by increasing the misery index they can cause the disadvantage to turn on each other while they blame the other political party for high crimes and gun violence. Many low-informational people of color and poor Whites have bought into their strategy, but millions understand the plot.

In the Georgia 2022 runoff, a Trump-backed candidate for the U.S. Senate, Herschel Walker, was rejected by thousands of Georgians. Even some Republicans rejected the idea of pitting a former Georgia Bulldog football player against an erudite Pastor of historic Ebenezer Baptist church, Raphael Warnock. Walker shamefully talked about werewolves, vampires, and bulls in heat while Senator Rev. Warnock talked about lowering the price of prescription drugs for seniors and working across the aisle to bring jobs and expand healthcare to the citizens. Republicans know that people of color can be used to take the edge off their racism while they carry out their harmful agenda. Thank God, it didn't work in the 2020 election.

African Americans have flexed their political muscles in key political races around the country. Perhaps this is why we are having so much trouble getting Congress to codify voting rights. In December of 2022 Congress passed, and the Biden Administration signed into law, the measures protecting same sex marriage and interracial marriage in lieu of a threat by the Right-wing leaning Supreme Court. I understand a "win is a win," but voting rights protection for African Americans have been illusive for well over a century or more. Blacks didn't have voting rights protection after 1877 or the Reconstruction period. Bloody Sunday occurred in Selma, Alabama in 1965 to obtain voting rights. It led to the passage of the Voting Rights Act, and if millions of our fellow citizens have anything to say about it, it will be an even longer time before we have protection.

African Americans cannot lose sight of our interests. We should take a page from Jewish leaders, and the leaders coming out of WW II who formed the North Atlantic Treaty Alliance (NATO) who established the rule that an attack on one is an attack on all of us. Even in our view toward the Continent of Africa. We should speak boldly against all forms of

American imperialism toward Africa. And we should work to build strong ties with mature African leaders who respect our interests. There are great possibilities lying before African Americans today. We must not allow anyone to rob us of these possibilities. We will have to look beyond the designs of this system which don't always have our best interests at heart.

This is my reflection on my journey while working in the field of civil rights. We must forge a new future for us and our children. I am committed to such an effort until I die.

Outside Looking In

The illusions of integration

Foreword

I was talking to my cousin Norman Banks, who pointed out some of my achievements. He said look at you. You are successful now compared to where you came from. I guess he had a point, but how do we measure success? I'm sure many have asked that question. My cousin reminded me that many people told us that he and I would never amount to anything, although they used a more vulgar language. We both had low self-esteem as children, but I always thought he was one of the coolest dudes I knew. Because he was a little on the heavy side, he earned the nickname Bear. Yet he had a rapport with some of the girls in the community, and man could he play basketball; more than that he has a heart as big as Texas.

Norman said I should give this book a title that reflected my accomplishments given all I've been through. I thanked him for the compliment and the advice. And I don't take my accomplishments lightly, but I can't allow myself to be lulled into a false sense of success. The truth is, we live in a country that regulates opportunities for certain people, and it is done through political policies. There are many achievements by black and brown Americans, but they have been minimized by those who tell U.S. history. I have come to see America as one big "plantation system."

As a boy I knew many Black people who had a credit account with stores. Through the week they would get food and other items on credit and settle on payday, which placed them back where they started – broke. I knew Black farmers who bought farm supplies on credit at the General Store, and if they had a bad crop year, their debt was compounded. Some even lost their land due to high debt. The managers of this system are ever modifying it to keep people of color on the bottom rung. We can't overlook the craftiness of those who hold sway over the financial and political power in this country.

Immediately after the Civil War 1865, the White landowners needed to get the former slaves back on the plantation to restore the Southern economy. They employed several tricks to do it; one such trick was the Black Codes, which was a set of laws that restricted the behavior of the newly freed men and women. One law allowed authorities to arrest and fine any Black person that was loitering in town and hire him/her out to a plantation owner to work off his debt. Women and children were made to serve as domestics to pay off their fines. My father told me about an incident that he witnessed in Florida around 1957 where Black people were arrested for loitering and sent to harvest citric fruits to pay off their fines. Today, we can still see the same spirit at work in those making state and federal laws. In Florida for instance, Gov. Ron DeSantis signed a House Bill 7, which bar schools and corporations from giving any instructions on discrimination, or as he put it, to stop wokeness in the workplace. According to DeSantis, "Florida is where wokeness comes to die." Even though the 1964 Civil Rights Act acknowledges a history of discrimination, DeSantis doesn't see a problem (Gov. Ron DeSantis campaign page). It has been said that those who forget the past are damned to repeat it. My view is that when we do not talk about, and reflect, on our history, we become vulnerable to political trickery.

A September 27, 2023, article by national digital reporter for Spectrum News, Joseph Konig revealed that Alabama Sen. Tommy Tuberville (R) is not in favor of equal opportunity in the military. He opposes Diversity, Equity, and Inclusion (DEI), or efforts to make the military a fair government entity. Said Tuberville, "Military is not an equal-opportunity employer." In fact, the military is an equal opportunity employer paid for by U.S. taxpayers. Tuberville, who previously coached the Auburn Tigers, once said at a Donald Trump rally that the descendants of Black slaves are criminals. His remarks were denounced by NAACP head Derrick Johnson. Many questioned whether he held these deep-seated sentiments about the Black players he coached. Only he and God know.

It's alright to send Americans of all races to fight and defend the nation, but they are not entitled to fair treatment in terms of promotions and assignments. People with a "plantation manager" mindset don't even hear their own logic or lack thereof. Clearly,

Tuberville is afraid that too many minorities may gain a meaningful influence over the U.S. military. He seems to think something must be done, to maintain the status quo.

Another good example of the "plantation system" is the music industry. Blacks figure prominently in the industry from blues, jazz, R&B, Pop, to Rap, but as Prince once put it, 50/50 is a partnership while 90/10 is employment. Black artists seem to always end up with the latter. In many fields, African Americans are paid less than their White counterparts.

Let's look at the transition. Percy R. Miller aka Master P sold thousands of dollars' worth of CDs out of the trunk of his car around 1993 (Wikipedia), but today a recording artist needs millions of streams on Spotify to earn a thousand dollars. Spotify, however, requires a $9.99 monthly subscription for the public to hear and stream the artist's music. The golden rule is in full effect, which says, the ones with the most gold make the rules. It is incumbent upon the exploited to fight against the "plantation managers" move against them. As Dr. Martin Luther King, Jr. once said, "Human progress never rolls in on wheels of inevitability; it comes through the tireless efforts and the persistent work of dedicated individuals who are willing to be co-workers with God. And without this hard work, time itself becomes an ally of the primitive forces of social stagnation."

Dr. Martin L. King Jr. once said, "I can't be what I ought to be until you are what you ought to be, and you can't be what you ought to be until I am what I ought to be because we are all tied together." Now I know to the individualist this is absurd. Such a position cannot stand alongside rugged individualism. And rugged individualism would be valid if it was universal. But it is not. For example, in 1862, prior to the Civil war, the Homestead Act was passed in the U.S. granting 160 acres of government land to any adult, provided they had not taken up arms against said government, and they did not labor in agriculture or domestic work, thereby locking out black and brown citizens.

That's not rugged individualism. That's plain old government assistance, the very thing that others accuse African Americans of getting on occasions. We have never had access to "white privilege," which means rugged individualism is all we've ever known. Since my birth I have beheld the struggle of black people in America, from the richest to the poorest while the bigots stood by looking down their noses at us. I took advantage of holes in the system that granted me certain opportunities, but I saw so many of my friends beaten down by that same system. I've been watching people survive on the scraps in a nation built by them and their ancestors. I dare not consider myself successful if there is no level playing field. Dr. King, Malcolm X, and many other people seeking justice were successful but did not see the change they were working for. We have always been "on the outside looking in." And to this day we have been grappling with the illusions of integration.

We have been told that this country was founded on the principle that "All men are created equal...," but we are treated otherwise. We pledge allegiance to the U.S. flag and say, "with liberty and justice for all," but each of us know that those words ring hollow for Black people. And any attempt by us to point out the obvious is met with hostility. We say, "Black Lives Matter" following the deaths of unarmed Black folks at the hands of police, but the opposition started chanting "All lives matter," or "blue lives matter." When we organize into protest groups of any kind, we are labeled a communist, or a socialist. And usually, the ones opposing us lean toward fascism, or just plain old White supremacy. Many Whites, who oppose us, feel that they must contain Black energy. They are afraid of the new possibilities we may usher in. Their worst fear is that the truth in all its glory may break forth in the land and bring about a new landscape in America. I hope that my story will be received by truth-loving people in such a way that it inspires personal development, hope, and a need to get involved with affecting change.

Birth

According to my birth certificate I was born on March 29, 1959, even though my last name is spelled wrong on the document (Wheller), I was given the name Joseph Wheeler after my father Joseph EJ Wheeler. That name was prominently held by Confederate General, Joseph Wheeler. Black people at the time generally took names from the Bible for their children. My paternal grandfather, Coma Wheeler is said to have come from Richmond County, Georgia near Augusta. Gen. Wheeler lived in that area also. I have yet to make any connection. Granddaddy looked White, and I've been told his father was White, but he didn't talk about him to dad and me. Mother said I was delivered with the help of a midwife at Aunt Lilly Mae's house 214 South Street in West Helena, Arkansas. She said she got up to use the slop jar, which was a pot used at night instead of going outside to the outhouse.

We lived with Aunt Lilly Mae. She did not have indoor plumbing at the time. Ms. Annie Mae Sikes was summoned to help bring me into the world. She had delivered countless babies in that town. Mother said it was very windy and cold that night. Because everyone in the household had to pull their own weight, a few weeks later, mother went off to the field to chop cotton or soybeans. This entails cutting the grass from around the cotton or soybeans. She left me with my ailing grandmother Florine. It was said that I was the apple of grandmother's eye. Unfortunately, she died before I could conceptualize her presence. She was 39. Two years later my mother gave birth to my sister Ella Ree (Rita) Miller. She was very light skin with sandy red hair. Mother never said who her father was.

My big brother, Jerreal Lee was already four years old by then. He and I were two years apart. Months later, the doctor found a spot on my mother's lungs. It turned out to be tuberculosis. She had to be quarantined in an institution in Little Rock about two hours away. Rita was sent to live with a hairdresser named Mary Lee Early. I often wondered why mother separated us. Was my sister a child born out of rape, or did my mother try to lessen the burden on Aunt Lilly Mae? Jerreal and I stayed with Aunt Lilly Mae. Sometimes we lived next door at Aunt Vannie's house. Both women were my grandmother's sisters. Aunt Lilly Mae's house consisted of her children Calvin, Will, Dollie Mae, Brenda, Earl Lee, James, and Jack (Jackie). Calvin, Will, Dollie, and Brenda were the older children. We were left under the charge of one of them in summer, while the others went to the field to chop cotton or soybean.

We didn't know it then, but our lives had been predetermined by a slave system designed long ago. Many Black people around us worked in the fields just as generations of Blacks did before them. Some managed to find work in other industries if they had education or some luck. But there was always work in the fields. If one could drive a tractor he could plow during plowing season. And at harvest time, the cotton needed picking for those landowners who didn't have a mechanical cotton picker. I recall seeing run-down houses in spots around the large cotton plantations on the back roads of Arkansas and Mississippi. Some are still there today. No doubt, these were the extension of the Negro quarters that existed during slavery. Most of the tenants were poverty stricken. They drew their water from a pump. We at least had a faucet in the yard, though no indoor plumbing.

Field work was back breaking. I knew many of the old people who walked with a stoop from years of working crouched over hoeing rows of cotton or soybeans, in addition to attending their own gardens to feed themselves. But times were changing. Machinery, pesticides, and other chemicals were making manual labor obsolete. And it couldn't come soon enough for my generation. Streams of Black people had been leaving the South to go up North for better opportunities. I recall hearing certain phrases among the elders that reflected this reality; when asked about a friend or relative the response would be "They went up the country," or "They went up North."

Aunt Lilly Mae, dressed in white during the week as she went to clean and cook for White people in "white town," which was the white section of West Helena. She would buy baby chicks for us to feed, candy and moon pies to sell, and seeds to grow vegetables in her garden. We all worked in the garden. We would shell peas, harvest corn, okra, sweet potatoes, tomatoes, and other vegetables. We fought with the hens to get eggs, and some days we would watch my older cousins cut off the necks of a rooster or a hen and dress it for supper. My Aunt Lilly Mae ran a tight ship. My older cousins had to join her in the field in the summertime. This extra money was used for school clothes and such. School was considered sacred to her. She herself only had maybe a sixth-grade education. But she taught us so much. She cooked many dishes, but my favorites were her flour bread, smothered fried chicken with gravy, candied yams, and a peach cobbler or blueberry pie for dessert.

She would tolerate no backtalk or misbehavior. When she said go and get a switch from the bush, we knew she meant a good strong switch, and she would mete out punishment from the oldest to the youngest. During the whippings all we heard was "Yes Madea! Yes Madea! Please Momma!" I ain't gone do it no more!" We dared not get caught laughing at the one getting punished, because that switch could easily turn on us. In summer the field bus would come and pick them up in front of the house, and off to work they went. After our chores, we smaller boys ran and played. Sometimes we would wander in our immediate surroundings and find plums, apples, dewberries, and apricots. These fruits grew all around us. Mr. Wilson lived next door. He had walnuts, apples, peaches and apricots. He would let us into the fenced-in yard to pick fruit at times. I later learned that he was the father of the lady who was keeping my sister. Everybody looked out for one another in our community. One day Mr. Wilson was sitting on the beautiful stairs leading to his yard complaining to my Aunt Vannie about a pain in his leg. Aunt Vannie went to her house and came back with coal oil. She poured it on his leg and it burst open. Soon little maggots started coming out. Gangrene had set in. Mr. Wilson had diabetes and had to have his leg amputated. Medical attention was not easy to come by because of prejudice and money. Home remedies worked for most ailments. Aunt Lilly Mae gave all the children castor oil and Black Draught. She kept a bottle of green alcohol in case one of us cut a finger or suffered some other bruises. As a child I enjoyed plenty of playtime, and I had my share of lumps and bruises.

My Aunt Lilly Mae managed to find some leisure time. Mr. J.B. Donaldson would stop by sometimes to see his sons. He also drove the field bus. All the children had to go outside and play when he came by. There was a certain song I use to hear coming from the window as Aunt Lilly Mae sang along, "We gonna pitch a ball to the wang dang doola ... All night long!" That was the one time I saw her take a drink of brown liquor. She believed in moderation. I loved seeing her happy with a big smile on her face. What good is life if all we did was work, I thought.

Cleanliness is next to godliness, and we had to wash clothes and keep the house clean daily. Her yard had no grass because we had worn it down. But Aunt Vannie's yard next door was a big contrast. It was green and well kept. She had two evergreen bushes opposite each other at the entrance to her driveway, and her hedges made a rectangle around her house. Her husband, Uncle Willie kept the yard and bushes manicured. Jackie and I loved to go onto the grass and wrestle. We had seen the wrestling matches on a TV set probably at Aunt Vannie's house because Aunt Lilly Mae didn't have a TV. At one time she didn't have electricity; however, things were starting to change.

Once, as Jackie and I wrestled on the grass, Aunt Vannie called out to me and said "Alright you little Sputnik. Bring your dusty ass in here and take a bath!" She had a colorful way of speaking. Sputnik Monroe was one of the wrestlers that we watched on TV. The matches took place in Memphis. Jackie laughed, and I earned a nick name. Everyone started calling me Sputnik. Many of my relatives thought it was very humorous, and they too started calling me Sputnik. Some do so to this day.

My Aunt Vannie was wealthy compared to most blacks around us. She and her husband had four or five rental houses, and they too, had gardens in the back of their house and some of their rental houses. Aunt Vannie worked for Bobby Brooks Clothing factory where they made women clothes. She always dressed impeccably when she went to church and other formal gatherings. She and Uncle Willie sang in the choir at True Vine Baptist church, where my brother and I had to say our Easter speeches every year. On some Sundays, the pastor would stop by for dinner. This was an auspicious occasion. Aunt Vannie and Uncle Willie was on their best behavior. At other times they argued back and forth. Auntie would make a pound or chocolate cake, macaroni and cheese, roast beef, or fried chicken, string beans, collard green and corn bread and to wash it down, she made sun-brewed tea with lemons. I loved it when the preacher came, so long as he didn't eat the choice pieces of the chicken. Aunt Vannie not only had a TV but a phonograph too.

She read the Helena World newspaper and watched Walter Cronkite religiously. She was well informed. One evening April 4,1968, I saw her face become flushed as the reporter announced the death of Dr. Martin Luther King Jr. She and Uncle Willie discussed the meaning of it, though to me it was just grown folks' stuff. Yet, I knew it was serious. Memphis was only about an hour and forty minutes away. Helenians went there all the time for business or medical treatment. The death of King sent tremors through our town.

I wanted to read like my cousins during this time. I was curious about a book they used to read to me. It was a story about several monkeys in a tree that would get caught in a rainstorm. They vowed to build a house to shelter them once the rain stopped. But when the sun came out, they went about playing happily like there was no tomorrow. But when the rain returned, they found themselves vowing once again to build a house when the rain stopped. I loved listening to my cousins read that book while looking at the pictures. It also stirred in me a hunger for more books. I was so excited when my Aunt Vannie began taking me to kindergarten around 1964.

Each morning, she would place a sandwich and an apple in my new red and green, plaid, book satchel. I can still smell the newness of that plastic satchel to this day. I would get into the front seat of her black Chrysler. She would have her radio station set on WDIA, a soul station out of Memphis. The Supremes would come across the airways singing My Baby Love or Stop! In the Name of Love, or one of the other Motown hits. We arrived at Ms. Bibbie's nursery school, a house which was no more than seven minutes away. My brother Jerreal was already attending Westside Elementary School. I tried to keep up with him and my cousins. Whatever they did I wanted to do, just like the typical annoying little brother. These were the days my Aunt Lilly Mae was whipping me for wetting the bed.

Every morning, she would come to my bed and check to see if the bed was wet. When it was, I was made to go outside in the cold and get a switch. I dreaded these mornings. Even Jerreal was starting to feel bad for me. He would wake me up in the middle of the night to go and pee. I was so grateful. These mornings were both dreadful and humiliating. I felt like a cursed child. None of the other children had this problem. That was my first great challenge in life. Other than that, childhood was great. My cousins introduced me to music also. We would string up wire on the back of the house and put cans under the wire to make musical sounds, or we would beat on large cans for drums.

On some Sunday mornings Aunt Vannie's son, James Carter and his group, the Pearlie Gates gospel quartet could be heard singing live on WDIA radio station. Auntie's smile said it all as they sang. She knew all the group members. I was very impressed also. She had copies of 45 records of her son and the group. James was the apple of her eye. I learned in later years that my Aunt Vannie had been raped and impregnated as a young teen by James' father around 1940. She gave the child to her sister Annie who was married to Ezell Bailey. She said she gave Annie and Ezell a mule and a wagon to keep James. I remember James coming by some Sunday afternoon in 1971 with his sons, James Jr., Robert, Julius, and Johnny. They would be dressed in their Sunday's best. James' daughter, Barbara Ann, stayed back with her mother Veola. They were a beautiful family, and Aunt Vannie was so proud of her son.

I learned just how close my family was as I grew and met them. My mother, her brother Percy Miller, James and all of Annie and Ezell's children played and worked in the field together when they were young. This close-knit village shielded my siblings and me as we grew. Vannie, Cannie, Annie, Ned, Eddie, my grandmother Florine were the children of an Indigenous man, Eugene Mathis Terry, and an African American woman named Mandy Vands. Eugene and Mandy came into the Arkansas territory from Mississippi. Aunt Vannie recounts the time when she and her siblings would ride in a horse-drawn wagon into downtown Helena to trade cotton for cloth to make their clothes.

Vannie said back in Mississippi, at night, Eugene had a certain call that he used to alert Mandy that he was approaching the house. I'm not sure why this Indigenous man adopted a European name and became a Christian. Eugene was probably born around 1887. I would think that some of his family members were affected by President Andrew Jackson's Indian Removal campaign, known as the Trail of Tears, which occurred between 1831-1850. Eugene went fishing one day according to his daughter, Vannie, and wrestled with a big bone buffalo fish in a tributary of the Mississippi River. After developing a lingering cough, he died a short time later. Vannie said he contracted tuberculosis. My grandmother Florine was born in 1920, the year her father died. Mandy Vands went on to have my grand aunt, Lilly Mae Minor, and her brother, Uncle Leroy Lockeridge. This is our clan.

I love my family dearly. They were all so hospitable, so welcoming even though they had their own unique challenges. Many of them were tied to agriculture early in life with little schooling but very ambitious hearts. Some went north to Chicago, Grand Rapids, or Detroit looking for better job opportunities even though a lot of money came through the twin cities, Helena and West Helena, during the late 1940s through the early 1970s. Helena was a hot blues spot right on the Mississippi River. The river boat would come through satisfying the appetite for gambling. Juke joints, liquor stores, and a beer brewery kept the workers liquored up on weekends. There were gambling houses, pool halls, a black movie theatre called the Plaza, owned by Eliza Miller, the one who built Eliza Miller High School for blacks in West Helena. The movie theatre stood next door to a black photography studio. There were boarding houses for out-of-town Black guests, and a Holiday Inn for white guests. Large Catholic churches, black and white protestant churches, and synagogues provided spiritual nourishment.

Soybean mills, cotton gins, the slab field, granaries, and other industries provided work. Both towns were booming economically. In West Helena, Chicago Lumber Mill was beginning to hire a great number of people in the community during the 1960s. I had several relatives who worked there. We lived in a wood frame shotgun house on Washington Street across from the mill around 1965. They called the houses shotgun because one could shoot through the front door and the bullet would go straight out the back door. They were very simple to construct.

We could see the men and women working at the mill from our house. There would be freshly cut trees stacked in rows near the road, prepared to be turned into lumber. Yellow Caterpillars would come and pick up the logs and transport them to the cutting areas. It was nothing to hear about a worker losing a finger or a limb on a wood saw there. black and white workers were segregated. They entered the mill through separate entrances where they clocked in. Whites parked in the left parking lot out front, and blacks parked on the right. There was a cafe that served the worker's lunch. They could also credit food there like spaghetti, tomato sauce, bread, cold cuts, pet milk, sugar, etc. It too was segregated.

My sister Ella Ree (Rita) was treated like a princess by Ms. Mary Lee. She bought her anything she needed or wanted. Mother had enough problems trying to feed Jerreal, herself, and me when she came home from the hospital, so Mary Lee's help was greatly appreciated. Mother was still sickly occasionally. Once, in the fall, my brother and I went with her to the field to pick cotton. The man gave her a long sack. He offered to pay her a dollar for each hundred-pound sack. My brother and I found that to be a near impossible task. We went down those cotton rows accumulating kookaburras in our hair and on our clothes. Today I can only imagine what a slave must have felt like picking all that cotton for free. Finally, my brother and I decided to put some large clogs of dirt in that sack to give it some weight. We took it back up to the truck to be weighed, but our plot was discovered. The man chided my mother to leave us at home the next time she came. That was the end of our cotton-picking experience.

Mother applied for welfare. We would soon be getting peanut butter, government cheese, powder eggs, powder milk, and pork in the can. A social worker came to the house to do an inspection. She looked in the chifforobe (closet), under the couch, and beds for a man's clothing and shoes. No man could be living in the house while she was receiving welfare. Now, this interference with relationships by the government was a double-edged sword. On the one hand, it did not encourage couples to live together, bond, and possibly marry. On the other hand, it gave some men an excuse to drop in and indulge in sexual pleasure with no commitment. If the couple married, the man's meager salary could barely sustain the whole family once the children started arriving; although, many black families made it work. Some black men, my father included, left town seeking better jobs and wages.

My mother was a beautiful slender built woman with long naturally wavy black hair. She had a deep brown skin tone, which reflected her Native American and African American roots. At an early age, I marveled at the way little girls competed for the opportunity to brush and comb my mother's hair. She savored every minute, sometimes almost falling asleep as they brushed, combed, and stroked her long black locks. Annie's daughters Ida (June), Cleola (Clee), Cornell (Nell), Pearlie Mae, Wadella (Wadie) and her son Ezell Jr. would figure prominently in my life once Momma returned from quarantine. They came to our aide with clothes, food, and encouragement.

Nell came down from Chicago and stayed with us until Mom gained her strength. Many Sundays, mother would dress us up and put us on that orange transit bus and travel to Helena Crossing to visit Aunt Pearlie Mae. Helena Crossing was so named because it was there that people crossed over the Mississippi River to go toward Tunica, or Clarksdale, Mississippi. Jerreal and I couldn't wait for the bus to stop. We would race to the back seat, not realizing that the back of the bus was designated for colored folks anyway. We just liked to watch the familiar sites disappear in the rear window. Mother shielded us from the Jim Crow do's and don'ts. Rarely, we went to public places except for the courthouse to get vaccinations.

When we arrived at Aunt Pearlie's house on those Sundays, we would greet her, Wadella, and Pearlie's husband, Isaac (Bud) Livingston. Aunt Pearlie's daughters would argue over who would get to comb my mother's hair first. But Jerreal and I couldn't wait to join Isaac Jr. across the street at Frankie Forman's house as they tinkered with their go carts. They rode these crude contraptions up and down that big hill like it was nobody's business. Eight-year-old Frankie and five-year-old Isaac were young engineers before we even knew what the word meant. They would take a wood board, thick electric cords, and old lawn mower tires and construct the meanest little go-car a kid could ever want. Jerreal and I got a thrill from riding those miniature race cars. We would beg mother on the weekend to take us to Aunt Pearlie's house just so we could ride on those go-cars.

Around this time in 1965, Mother had met a Chicago Mill worker named Roosevelt Kemp, a stocky, dark-skinned man with a receding hair line. This union produced my brothers Michael and James Kemp. Three other children, Sherneece, Linda, and a stillborn son died in infancy later. Roosevelt started by visiting us occasionally. He tried to win favor with my brother and me by giving us a dime or a quarter. It worked. We bought marbles, spinning tops, yoyos, and candy all the time now. He finally moved in, but he had to be careful not to leave any male clothing behind. We learned early how to lie to white folks when they questioned us. Sometimes mother would have us tell the rent man she wasn't home when she couldn't pay the rent, but overall, this was a happy time for my brother and me mainly because we had reunited with our mother, and we didn't have to live with relatives.

While I was curious about my father, he was out of sight out of mind. We saw him once when we lived with Aunt Vannie. She called my brother and me over one day in 1964 and pointed to a man dumping someone's garbage into the West Helena Sanitation truck. We ran down there at my aunt's prompting and introduced ourselves. He was a light-skinned, slender built, man with hazel eyes. He seemed rather detached from us, but he did acknowledge that he was our father. He reached into his pocket and gave each of us a dime. I was excited to meet my father for the first time. This could be the beginning of something new, I felt. But Jerreal could care less one way or the other. I was five then and Jerreal was seven. Unfortunately, I would be nine before I saw him again.

On that next encounter (1968) Dad took me to Marianna, Arkansas to stay with him for short spans. But suddenly without notice, Daddy would go back up North. I ran errands for his brother's grandmother, Mrs. Annie Miles, when I was five. Mrs. Miles, who lived two houses away, showered me with love even though I didn't quite know how we were related. I needed a grandmother, so I adopted her, and her grandsons became my uncles. Jerreal and me along with neighbors, Nathan and Jackie Ray Robinson loved throwing rocks across the street to the logs at Chicago Mill. But at times Mrs. Miles would scold us about it, and she did so with great authority. We said yes ma'am and found a new game. She felt like a very close relative to me. I became her favorite and she mine.

Roosevelt had an account with the Chicago Mill Cafe. At times mother would send Jerreal and me to buy food items on his account. Jerreal and I learned early how to add two honey buns and root beer sodas to mother's list. Jerreal matched mother's handwriting closely. A young white guy Little Joe, and his female companion Katherine managed the place. They were entertained by watching me and my brother arm wrestle. My brother would out best me most times. We won favor with them. That was my first close interaction with white people; a year later I would meet whites my age, and it wasn't so pleasant. It was after we moved to Little Rock Road across the street from Oak Grove Cemetery. Behind our double tenant brick house was an open cotton field that stretched for about a half of mile. West of our row of houses was a fenced off area that contained a nice house, a tractor shed, a horse stable, and two beautiful ponies. I used to go over and feed them grass that I pulled up near the fence. They were very friendly and seemed to look forward to my coming. One day I ventured to the entrance way of this area and met two blond-haired boys, each of them was riding one of the ponies. They had bottles of orange Fanta sodas. As I drew near, one of them spewed out his soda on me. They laughed, and the other boy did the same. Soon they were calling me names. Something inside me told me that they were privileged. While I was very angry, I restrained myself and made my way back to my house next door. They rode their horses past my house on the road. I pondered what had happened. Clearly, they lived in a separate world from mine, and I could not process the difference at the time.

At the Chicago Mill Cafe, we had to enter through the colored side door, which seemed normal to me at the time. I must have been around 6 years old. Occasionally, we would be there as the black mill workers filed in for lunch and filled up the rows of swivel stools that made a U shape around the long beige counter. Little Joe would take their orders. The wood floor was bare and a dark ebony color, a great contrast to the side of the cafe, which was air conditioned, noticeably cleaner, with a bright color white linoleum rug on the floor and pictures of nature and hunting on the wall. I was experiencing Jim Crow but was not fully aware of it. I was, in the words of W.E.B. Dubois, living life behind the veil.

My mother, stepfather, brothers, aunts, uncles, and the elders insulated me. My mind was occupied with neighborhood friends, TV shows with predominantly white characters, and soul music on the radio. Cowboys and Indians movies were our favorites. We viewed the red man as a vicious savage, not knowing at the time my great grandfather was an indigenous man, and my mother, his granddaughter, bore his features. Mother didn't know much about her indigenous grandfather, at least she never mentioned him to us. I would learn about him many years later from Aunt Vannie. I don't know where Eugene Mathis Terry is buried, but the black cemetery, Oak Grove, where Florine is buried, was a dear place to me. It was well kept by a man named Mr. Hosea. There weren't many graves there when I was a child. Grandmother Florine's grave is marked by an upside-down Coke bottle next to her undertaker husband Mr. Clemons. The latter had a tombstone, but not his wife, probably because the family couldn't afford one. We would play baseball or football on the freshly cut grass field where there were no graves.

On some paydays my brother and I would stand at the exit to the mill and wait for a relative or two to come out so we could bum a dime or a quarter. We had to be very discreet about it, because certain elders would scold us for begging and threaten to tell our mother. Begging was frowned upon in our community. Ms. Miles' grandson Bullet didn't mind giving us a dime or more, and there were others we felt comfortable approaching. With about 15 cents in hand, we were off to C.P. Lewis or a Chinaman store to buy marbles. We loved playing with marbles. Jerreal was the best shooter. He would win all the neighbors' marbles including mine. I was average. Jerreal was big enough to walk to school alone, but I got lost just trying to go to Toy Store (the Chinese name) a block over from my house. My sense of direction was terrible. I had no problem going to C.P. Lewis for Ms. Miles because I went there often.

Ms. Miles was the mother of Pete Miles. I met Pete when he lived with some relatives next to Oak Grove Cemetery. He sat in a chair, and his eyes blinked as if he had been through some traumatic experience. He had a constant twitch, and his limbs jerked. I was told that he was shell shocked after being wounded in WW II. Pete had some children by my paternal grandmother Lucille Grover, one of which was my uncle Genie. We were family as far as Ms. Miles was concerned.

I loved Ms. Miles and her grandsons, Bullet and Willie. Willie had a beard like the man on the Prince Albert Tobacco can. He went to the dentist to get a tooth pulled one day and developed continuous bleeding. He bled to death. I saw the ambulance come and carry his body out of the house. That was my first encounter with death around 1965. It was a dreadful feeling. My brother, neighborhood friends, and I talked about it for a while. Ms. Miles who walked with a stoop could be seen in her front yard gathering wood to cook with after Willie's death. I would run over to help her and try to console her. She explained to me how she tried to get him to go back to the doctor, but he would not go. A nephew, Ethelman, lived with her also. He took it all in stride. He was a sharp dresser who loved to drink Golden Rod wine and listen to his transistor radio. He was crazy about Chuck Berry's song Memphis Tennessee, a song that came out the year I was born.

During this time, I started listening to songs by Sam Cooke, Otis Redding, Rufus Thomas, and Bobby Blue Bland. I was hearing Momma sing around the house with the songs on the radio as she cleaned and cooked. Music was everywhere now. I loved hearing

my mother sing in perfect pitch. I started singing too.
My brother sang a little but not with the enthusiasm
that Momma and I had. My neighbors next door had a
phonograph. Listening to the same records over again
afforded me the opportunity to learn the lyrics and the
melody. Soon I was trying to sing every day.

On Fridays, mother would make hamburgers, and
we would watch the Flintstones on the TV Roosevelt
bought for us. Each Friday night, Mother would watch
Fantastic Future. That was a very scary show to me,
just the intro music alone would strike fear in my
heart. She enjoyed it and that meant so much to me.
I'd have to leave the room until I mastered my fear.
We learned to appreciate TV shows and movies
through our mother. She would explain them whether
it was I Love Lucy, The McCoy's, The Rifleman,
Imitation of Life, or Tarzan. Jerreal and I preferred
cowboys and Indian movies. Little did we know at the
time we were internalizing stereotypes about the
Indigenous people, and black people too. We would
mock each other and our friends calling them Ju Ju,
and nappy-headed niggers. It was so funny at the
time, but we were subtly developing a mild self-
hatred.

Roosevelt got paid on Fridays. He bought groceries,
paid the bills, and then he was off to the carline to
gamble and drink gin. The carline was so named
because cars would line the black side of Plaza Street
in front of the juke joints, gambling houses, and the
one liquor store called Alps. Black men and women

were drawn to these spots like a magnet to drink, gamble, and forget their troubles for a little while. Alps' liquor store stood on one end of the black side of Plaza Street, and the Powerhouse church stood on the opposite end. True Vine, First Baptist, Greater First Baptist, an AME church, and Second Baptist Church all provided spiritual nourishment for the people. There were juke joints like Hots, Degos, Shannon, and ABC. Radio James had the main gambling spot, but there were others.

Sometimes Roosevelt wouldn't come home on payday. We would be waiting, with our stomachs growling from hunger. One Friday evening, he did not show up at all. Saturday morning, he arrived broke with a hangover. I'm not sure what kind of conversation he and Momma had, but Roosevelt improved his behavior. In fact, he and Momma began dressing up and dressing us up for church on Sundays. It turned out that Roosevelt was a friend of Rev. Holland who also worked at Chicago Mill. Holland would baptize my brother and me at Lakeview, Arkansas.

I would see many of these mill workers at the churches we frequented. I also learned that Chuck Berry, James Brown, Sam Cooke and the others I heard on the radio were singing Devil's music. I could hear the difference between the sacred church music and the devilish secular music, but I loved the latter better. Plus, when I saw Jackie Wilson or James Brown on the Ed Sullivan Show, I was mesmerized by their talent. The energy from that music was so powerful. Luckily my mother wasn't so strict about what we listened to. Roosevelt's mother Mrs. Ethel and his father Mr. Aaron Kemp were devout Christians who read the Bible fervently. They had the ideal Christian home. Mr. Aaron Kemp served in WW II. He could be seen often walking up to the American Legion Hut where they hosted community events to raise money for the veterans. He was engaged in civic activities from voting to community meetings, and very active at his church. He wore his WW II garrison cap with great pride.

Gradually I became very curious about religion. I began to understand more about this dichotomy between the church folks and the sinners in our community. I saw so many elders who walked in humility and Christian character, and then I saw some who loved hanging out on the carline on weekends and some weekdays too. At times I would see men and women drunk out of their minds at the juke joints listening to BB King, Muddy Waters, and Bobby Blue Bland. They would be drinking and dancing their troubles away it seemed. I saw a person or two in the neighborhood drunk. It seemed that they had given up on life. I knew that wasn't what I wanted out of life. West Helena was bustling with activity. H&H Lumber Company was our version of Home Depot back then. It stood between the Black and White sides of Plaza Street. Local businesses Mohawk and Doughboys had the highest paying jobs for blacks. Many blacks worked at McKnight Mill, and West Helena Chemical

Company.

We had several stores on the Black side of town, five of which were Chinese-owned, and seven were Black-owned. There was a community garden behind those shotgun houses where all the tenants worked just as we did at my Aunt Lilly Mae's house. I remember eating cucumbers and tomatoes from that garden. The flavor of these vegetables and vinegar reminds me of my mother to this day. The Black-owned C.P. Lewis, Kid Gray, Molene, the Buccaneer, and Snowball stores served our immediate community. Wang, Pang, Toy, Frank Jo, and Johnny's were Chinese-owned grocers which served the broader black community as the town was segregated.

Black owned Hopkins and John Henry stores served the black community on the southside. The Chinese Exclusion Act of 1882 had a lasting impact on Chinese Americans and their status in this country. It was meant to stop Chinese from migrating to the U.S. and to keep Chinese Americans here from becoming naturalized citizens. Their children were not allowed to go to school with white kids or live in white communities, which might explain why they were in the black community. The Statue of Liberty says "send me your tired and teaming masses," but historically that did not include Chinese or most other non-whites.

We enjoyed a harmonious relationship with the Chinese for the most part. There were occasions when black farmers collaborated with Chinese store owners. I remember buying products from all of them. My Aunt Vannie had a friendship with one Chinese family that lasted until her death. They would send her birthday and Christmas cards every year. To most blacks, the Chinese people were victims of discrimination just as we were. We made the best of our situation. Only the most educated knew about the Chinese Exclusion Act. Most in my family certainly did not.

On Easter Sunday, West Helena would come alive with people wearing the most beautiful colors. Church houses would be full. You would see people there who had not gone to church all year. Mother would have my brother and me practice our Easter speeches. We would stay up late at night practicing, and coloring Easter eggs, anticipating the egg hunt and church activity on Easter. At church, saying our speeches was sometimes a formidable challenge if you had a long one. I resented getting a short one. Although I was very shy, sometimes I would surprise myself by how well I delivered the speech. And then sometimes I'd bum?. Receiving praise from the elders was so magical. Occasionally, one would slip me a nickel or a quarter. I associated that praise with the virtues of education. I wanted to get that kind of praise all the time. I would get more opportunities later when I attended school. Clearly, there was a class of black folks spearheading efforts to bring progress to our community.

I can write a chapter on the work and influence of light skinned blacks in Helena-West Helena. Yes, skin color affected us too. I used to hear bits and pieces about Mrs. Eliza Miller, who could almost pass for White. Indeed, there were quite a few fair-skinned black professionals, referred to as mulattoes, but that's a derogatory term. They were of mixed heritage, however, like the Stephens who owned Stephens Funeral Home, Jackson Highley, who owned a funeral parlor, the physician Dr. Miller, educators Florine and Roland Buchanan, the Alexanders and others. Mrs. Florine Buchanan stood out for me. I heard my mother, stepfather, and other grown folks praise the Buchanans for the work they were doing in education. Some of the elders mis-pronounced their names out of ignorance. They called the husband, Professor Buck-anna. That was a household name.

One could see the influences of both W.E.B. Dubois' talented tenth strategy and Booker T. Washington's self-help program working side by side. Dubois had suggested that the talented 10% of black people should lead the masses of black people as the community developed. This should involve voting and fending for our rights under the U.S. Constitution. Washington proposed that black folks should focus on agriculture, owning land, learning vocations, and building our community without unnecessary confrontations with Caucasians. No one simply waited on government handouts. Most black adults were engaged in some type of industry and seeking to increase their fortunes. But some joined unions to fight for equal pay. The Massacre in Elaine, Arkansas of 1919 had to do with peonage abuses among the black tenant farmers. It is believed that 100-237 blacks and 5 whites were killed in the massacre. Avoiding confrontations with a system designed for and controlled by Whites is constant.

Peonage was very much tied to sharecropping and debt slavery or debt servitude, which is a system where an employer compels a worker to pay off a debt with work. Legally, peonage was outlawed by Congress in 1867, but that did not mean it necessarily stopped.

Again, life in West Helena was bustling. While the wages for black workers were much lower than that of white workers, employment was improving with the arrival of Chicago Mill Lumber Mill. As mentioned, there were separate entrances, but the black workers were just glad to have jobs. Some black workers would get their paycheck on Friday and end up on the carline that evening. All along the strip you could hear the latest blues songs by Albert King, Muddy Waters, BB King, Bobby Blue Bland, and others. I am told that Alp's liquor store owner served multiple purposes. In addition to selling liquor, he cashed checks, and provided high interest loans. Black-owned Shannon pool hall was another source of high interest loans. Mr. Shannon had a reputation for packing a pistol and selling bootleg whiskey on Sunday. He also allowed gambling in the back room. I can only imagine the hoops the established banks made Black folks jump through to get a loan.

Education was something most Black Helenian adults craved. And some felt that since they didn't attain it, they would ensure that their children did.

In 1969 I started school. It was a major challenge for Momma and me at first. She had to send off for my birth certificate which took forever it seemed, and I had to get vaccinated. Finally, at ten years old I was in school at West Side Elementary. It was very awkward at first. There I was with six-year-olds trying to explain to them why I was so big and in the first grade. Lucky for me there were a couple of other kids who started late also. In later years my father revealed to me that he was thirteen years old when he started school, and he dropped out in the second grade. He made many attempts over the years to become functionally literate but to little avail. I could certainly identify with his struggle.

Mrs. Buchanan saw my challenge early on and zeroed in on me just like she had done with my father and mother. This said a lot about her commitment to educating the black population. It would be about a month before she died (2003) that she told me how her career began. She said that she was trained at a school in Mississippi that had been set up by the Freedmen Bureau decades prior. White missionaries came from the North to set up these schools to train Black educators so they could teach the newly freed slaves. So, Mrs. Buchanan and her loving husband Roland were what we called (removed 'a') "race man and woman" in that they were concerned about the progress of the race.

Mrs. Buchanan instructed us to bring a big brown shopping bag to school so we could write our names on them and hang them under the chalk board at the front of the class. All our schoolwork would be placed into this bag. A month later there was an Open House where the parents came to see their children's work. Mother didn't come. I noticed the other parents and their children smiling over their progress. Mrs. Buchanan made me her helper, giving me a sense of importance in the classroom. One day during some down time, she came by my desk and caught me drawing a picture. She said surprisingly, "Joseph, I didn't know you could draw!" Soon she had me drawing fall pictures on her bulletin board. She would parade the other teachers into her room to see my work, and they started requesting to use me to draw on their bulletin boards. The other students would look on in amazement until the teacher would have them turn around and focus on their work; meanwhile, my ego was swelling up from all the attention. She saw something in me, and that meant so much. Thank you Mrs. Buchanan.

One day Mrs. Buchanan confronted me. She had instructed me to be under the table reading when she came in each morning. I was running around the classroom playing with the other kids when she called my name in a mean parent's voice "Joseph Wheeler!" she screamed, "I thought I told you to be under that table reading when I came in!" She looked at me while squinting with one eye, bearing a frown on her face. She waddled to her desk carrying her bags of school supplies. Mrs. Buchanan was an obese woman. I froze. She said, "Come here!" as she took her seat and pulled her black fan belt from her top drawer. I had seen her beat the hands of other students. I had even seen her raise the young girls' dresses up and spank them on their bottoms, but I thought we had a special relationship. After all, she had given me some of her husband's old clothes and shoes. I had picked dandelions to give to her and her mother when I passed by her mother's house some evenings. Didn't that count for anything? She looked me in the eyes with a stern look as I held out my hand for punishment, and said "You are just like your father, slothful, and hardheaded, but I'm going to break you up from that. When I tell you to get under that table and read you had better do so!" "Yes mam," I said. And she beat my hand until it turned blood red. I cried and went to my seat. She said, "Get under the table and read until I call you." "Yes ma'am," I said weeping all the while, and embarrassed. And I was under that table reading every morning after that.

My reading and comprehension soared under her program. In fact, I started going through the Jack and Janet series, level one, two, three, etc., and before I knew it, I was reading second grade material, and doing just as well in math. My learning accelerated. Toward the end of the school year Mrs. Buchanan took me to Second Grade teacher, Mrs. Billingsley's room to show her my progress. Mrs. Billingsley was impressed. She declared, "He doesn't need to come to the second grade, skip him to the third grade." After scoring so high on the second-grade test, I was promoted to the third grade. I felt so good. At least I was only three years behind in school now.

In the third grade, I was under the charge of Mrs. Lee Esther Johnson, another highly esteemed figure in our community. She taught us English. I still had a challenge with decent school clothes especially around kids whose parents seemed to be well off economically. Torin Corbin, Dorletha Dentmon, Eric Bailey, Debbie and Marjorie Boyland, and the beautiful Jacqueline Holloway were some of my classmates at this time. I was infatuated with a beautiful bright-skinned girl named Sylvia Collins. She was sassy and cute. She wore her hair in a ponytail. I believe my heart skipped a beat every time I came close to her. These were powerful feelings and very new. I used to write little love notes, saying I love you. Do you love me? She would make a leave-me-alone face at me. But I wouldn't give up. I kept trying to impress her, but she gravitated more toward the sharply dressed Torin Corbin. He had the pick of all the little girls it seemed; however, he didn't care a thing about Sylvia. Man, if I could be so lucky. Maybe it was the clothes. Torin was very neat, his hair well groomed, and he had personality.

I had low self-esteem, inadequate school clothes, and the third-grade teachers had little use for an artist. I continued to draw pictures at my desk. Even Sylvia had me draw something for her. Some of the guys thought I was very talented. If only they had a school dance, I could show them how well I could do some James Brown moves. My relatives and neighbors would seek me out at family gatherings just to dance for them. My classmates had not met that side of me yet. Opportunities for public dance were rare for kids my age. Sometimes the high schoolers would have functions involving music and dance. Everyone in our town has heard about Tenneson Price. Once, I got a chance to see him in action. He had the moves that would have impressed even James himself. The first sound of Papa's Got a Brand-New Bag, Tenneson would hit the floor and have everyone mesmerized. He was just that good. He inspired many of us young boys.

During the summer months in 1970, I started maintaining the yard and flowers at Mrs. Lee Esther Johnson's house. Apparently, her adopted son Allen Sheard was tired of doing the work, and he had football practice at Central High School. Mrs. Johnson would pull up in her luxurious car and nod her head with approval as she unloaded household items from her car. One evening she called me over from the makeshift basketball dirt court across the street and gave me a large shopping bag filled with brand new shirts, pants, and shoes. I guess she took pity on me and my raggedy school clothes. I was so grateful. Allen and his sister Rose Mary became my dear friends. Allen got all the nice things a kid could want, a five-speed bike, boxing gloves, basketballs, footballs, football uniforms, and all the things we could not afford; yet there was never any arrogance among this family. No boasting.

Mr. Johnson was a farmer who owned acres of land in Cattaca Bottom, Arkansas along with heads of cows, and hogs. Allen talked Jerreal and me into going to the Bottom with him to help slop hogs and chop soybean. He asked us to join him mainly because he wanted company, but also to help him finish the work quickly to return to playing street football. He was obsessed with sports. This was back-breaking work; however, but Allen knew how to make fun of everything. He called Jerreal and me over to a bull, as he would put the palm of his hand on the animal's forehead. The bull charged him, and he would run to the wood fence and climb over it just in time.

Later, Allen would aggravate a sow (female hog) in the hog pen. That sow would come charging and we all took off running. After a while, Mr. Johnson would call out, "Allen stop that playing and get back to work!" We mended barb wire fences, and shoveled hog feed off the back of Mr. Johnson's truck. Sometimes we'd haul barrels of watermelon rinds and old food on that truck. Riding on the back of that truck with the wind hitting our faces was the highlight of the whole workday. Mr. Johnson always fed us, and sometimes he gave Jerreal and me a few dollars. They lived in one of the finest brick houses on our side of town. They even had a piano. I learned to play my first song on it, Lean on Me by Bill Withers.

I spent a lot of time at the Johnson's hanging out with Allen, and lusting at his beautiful sister Rose Mary who was as fine as Thelma on the sitcom, Good Times. She had the prettiest legs, and the sweetest laugh. I was in love though she was much older than Allen and me. Allen used to brag about his big brother having served in Vietnam. I met him one day on the carline. He held his arm as though it was in a sling. He showed us where he had received shrapnel in his arm from some type of bomb. He appeared beaten down in spirit, very withdrawn. I felt sorry for him. Allen thought he was a hero, and I guess, in a sense he was. There were many older guys in our town who walked around wearing their Army shirts, jackets, or caps signifying that they had served. Songs like Curtis Mayfield Back to the World, Joe Tex song about Jackie Robinson, Marvin Gaye What's Going On, and other war era songs were their favorites, and mine too even though I didn't fully understand the current events at the time.

The Weekly Reader papers we discussed in Mrs. Johnson's class did help me a little. I saw my nickname in one of these papers as we talked about Sputnik I, a Russian satellite that had been launched into space. I understood the Apollo missions and the space race between the United States and Russia. The paper never mentioned Katherine Johnson, the black female mathematician who helped calculate the distance and aided the successful mission of the spacecraft. Many of the black people I knew thought it was white folks' business and nothing more. As Malcolm X once said when he heard a black person refer to the astronauts as "our astronauts," he remarked, "They won't even let black folks near the plant." The 2016 movie "Hidden Figures" tells the story of the first African American women to work at NASA during the Space Race. Each woman featured in the movie had important responsibilities.

Many of the young black men viewed the Vietnam war as a senseless war in which poor people lost the most. black power symbols were everywhere during these days. The Jackson 5 figured prominently with their big afros. Don Cornelius, and the Soul Train dancers all wore afros and afro puffs, bell bottoms and stack heel shoes and daishikis. Young people were breaking with the old mores of the times. Black was beautiful. It was all about being hip or aware. Today they call it being woke. The Jeffersons, Good Times, Red Foxx, had broken through the big screen. And whitey was the man. Fat Albert and the Jackson 5 cartoons were the kids favorites even though we still watched the other cartoons. Something was happening.

The winds of change were blowing. Arguments broke out when parents tried to get their boys to cut off their afros, and "look decent." To us our afros were decent and black! We remained respectful to the elders and the generations that came before us, but it was time to do something different. Richard Pryor was criticizing white folks to their faces and even they were laughing. Jim Brown, Fred Williamson, Paul Whitfield, Cicely Tyson, Pam Greer, Muhammad Ali, and other black athletes and entertainers were giant icons on the big screen. Allen and so many of my childhood friends would hold long conversations about these heroes and heroines and about our local Vietnam heroes.

I never learned why Allen and his sister lived with Mr. and Mrs. Johnson or what their relationship to them was. Allen's father lived in a house on Plaza Street (the carline), and he stayed intoxicated. Allen and I would visit him occasionally. He was very polite. He spoke well of Allen, but then because of the alcohol, his conversation would deteriorate into something else. I thought about this around 2004 when I came home to visit. I ran into Allen. He was working for the Helena hospital. His marriage was on the rocks, and he had been drinking. We reminisced about our childhood and his brilliant performance on the Central High football team. But when his eyes turned away, and he stared into the distance, I could tell that he was grappling with a pain so deep. He talked about getting his wife and children back. He asked me if I would give him a ride to the liquor store. I said "Yes. Hop in!" We changed the subject again, as we rode along. We recalled old friends and what they were doing nowadays, as we laughed and talked. I didn't realize that this would be the last time I would see him. Someone told me a few months later he was struck by a car on the highway. I remember wishing that I could have said something to alter the course that he was on. He was such a good-natured, intelligent, human being. I forgot to thank him for all the good times and love he gave to my brother and me as kids. He had it all, but never acted snobbish.

Meeting white kids introduced me to some new experiences, some good, and some not so good. For example, during the fourth grade 1971 I walked home from school along with some of the white kids. I met a poor white guy named Dwayne Phillips. He had dishwater, blond hair, and blue eyes. He had an "I don't care attitude." We introduced ourselves, and he pulled out a cigarette and began smoking like a grown man. First, a ten-year-old smoking in public was frowned upon by the elders on my side of town, but this guy had no fear. I talked him into going down an alley with me and showing me how to smoke. I would steal cigarettes from my mother and meet him in the alley after school. It took me a while. I coughed my head off the first few tries, but soon I was inhaling the smoke and blowing it out like a pro. Dwayne was bad news on his side of town. I was told later that he was sent to reform school. I stopped seeing him at our school before the school year was over.

In the fourth grade, I signed up to be a crossing guard along with a white student, Robert Bailey. We got to school early to get our badges, helmets, and florescent orange waist and shoulder harnesses along with our bamboo flag poles. We stood at the intersection and stopped the cars to let the children cross until school took up for class. We were like disciplined soldiers on our post. In the evening, we returned to do it again. We felt important like real police officers. Looking back, my early experience as a crossing guard affected a later decision to become an MP in the Army.

After school, Robert's father would give us a ride home on the back of his truck. Robert was one of the nicest white guys I had met during these days. His father would take us to the Buccaneer for hamburgers and shakes. This black-owned burger stand had the best burgers and shakes in town. Mr. Bailey renamed it the "purple cow" because the building was purple. On some days Mr. Bailey would take me to their house so I could play with Robert. He liked building model airplanes by gluing the parts together. Sometimes we would wonder over to their small neighborhood store. His mother would be there behind the counter. She would tell us to get a bag of chips and a soda, or whatever we liked. I had never seen such a privilege. Their house was a beautiful red brick structure with a fireplace. Robert and his sister had their own rooms. Outside there was a spacious manicured backyard where we played catch ball. One day some guys from the neighborhood came over to play football. A couple of them made every effort to hurt me when I ran the ball. It wasn't long before they started slanging the n-word around, and Robert felt it was time to end the game and go inside. I heard the word "nigger lover!" as Robert and I walked away with the ball. I remember feeling I had brought tension between him and his friends. He had to live in that neighborhood after I returned home. I had arguments and fights with kids in my neighborhood before. Generally, we would wrestle each other to the ground, or throw a lick or two and be done with it. We would be friends the next day. But this was a different kind of dispute. I couldn't quite process it at the time.

One day I got to school, and Robert didn't show up. I wondered what had happened. I didn't have a phone to call him, so I took it upon myself to walk the ten blocks or so to his house. It was a journey. I crossed the railroad tracks into "white town," which is what we called their section. I went past the big White church on Plaza Street, and took a left by Beech Crest elementary school, previously an all-white school. And then I took another right and counted the blocks, 4th street, 5th street etc., but somewhere around 8th street just as I was walking in front of a corner house, a bald man with a pot-gut walked out on to his front porch. He wore black framed glasses. His face was red with anger. I soon realized he was the owner of West Helena Furniture Company from whom my mother and many other black people I knew rented furniture. He screamed out "Hey nigger what are you doing in this neighborhood?" I was speechless. What law had I broken? Was it a law that I wasn't told about?

I remember walking away real fast, not sure of what would happen next. I was too close to Robert's house to turn around. But I didn't feel safe where I was, so I stepped up my pace. I could hear the man hurling obscenities at me "Don't let me catch your nigger ass over here again! you hear me!?" I passed 9th street and finally made it to 10th street and seeing that familiar red brick house brought me some comfort. I ran to the door not knowing whether the furniture man was following me in his vehicle. I knocked on the door looking back all the while. Mr. Buddy opened it and said, "Oh hi Joe, you must be looking for Robert?" I said, "yes sir." He said "come on in. Robert was sick today. That's why he didn't come to school."

Robert walked down the hall with a smile on his face but looking a bit weak. We went to his room where he was gluing parts of his airplane together. I felt the need to rehearse in mind about my ordeal with the furniture guy to Mr. Buddy. I was hoping that he would drive down there and give him a piece of his mind. But he just sat me down and said "You know Joe, there are some bigots in this world that think they are better than others. And you just have to ignore their type." I listened respectfully as he explained that world of bigots, but I was sensing that it was not a major problem for him and his family, but this bigot was the one who rented furniture to my family and many other black people I knew.

I remember thinking to myself, "Is that it?" "No man-to-man talk with this guy who threatened a guest of your son?" Suddenly I felt that this was an exclusive society, and I was an outsider who wasn't completely accepted. When it was time to leave, I asked Mr.

Bailey for a ride home. I was afraid to pass this man's house. What if there were others who were more ruthless than our furniture man waiting for me? I didn't want to take that chance. I never returned to Robert's house again though we remained friends.

I looked Robert up one day around 2009. But his mother told me that he passed away from some disease. Robert and I had a genuine friendship, and our job as patrol boys at school put us in a different category from the rest. He was a constant reminder to me over the years that children, if left alone, can be decent human beings. But social, political, and economic forces play a great role in keeping this system of hatred in place. I learned also that the fear of losing power and privilege can breed racial hatred. Those who enjoy the privilege structural racism brings have no real incentive to change the system.

I met another white friend in the fourth grade named Kenny Yates. He used to love to go down the short alley way to Hopkins store to buy Now or Later candy. I did too, except I couldn't afford them every day. But Kenny could. He was loaded with dough. And some of the black bullies knew it. It wasn't long before guys began to take his lunch money. I happened to witness them one day as they were roughing up Yates. A black boy had him by the collar and told him to give him his money. I intervened. I said, "Let my friend go, or it's gone be me and you!" The bully called my bluff, but I was bigger and more determined. Kenny thanked me profusely, and announced, "You are my best friend." I got free Now or Later candy every day, and Kenny and I became childhood friends.

I always had a soft spot for the underdog. And I hated those who bullied others regardless of race. Maybe that came from being socialized by the TV. I wasn't sure what that cost me with my black friends. At that time, we were suspicious of black students who were caught talking like whites or acting like whites. We would call them Oreo cookies, black on the outside and white on the inside. This saying was passed down to us by the Central High School black students. They had riots at that school when school first integrated. Again, we were in one big experiment. I was informed about race by my peers, high schoolers, and black and white adults. Yet, I was still confused.

Prominent black educators like school superintendent Roland Buchannan, his wife Florine, Principal Lloyd and Mrs. Debra Black, Mrs. Lee Esther Johnson, Ms. Chambers, Mrs. Kirkland, Mr. Williams, M. Chapman, Mrs. Valentine, Mrs. Youngs, Mrs. Billingsley, and Mrs. Clark were royalty in our community. There were two things most of the elders stressed - faith in God, and education. Being able to read, write, and do arithmetic was something many of the elders did not get the chance to achieve. Working in the fields kept them from attending school much of the time. My mother only obtained a seventh- grade education, and my father dropped out in the second grade. I watched them struggle with reading and writing.

The pressures of life forced them to drop out. I learned better at the segregated school than I did when school integrated. In 1971 my whole academic world was upended. I went from having teachers who nourished, taught, and disciplined me to teachers who seemed indifferent. The white teachers who came to Westside that year appeared to bond well with the white students. I felt like I was part of an experiment. We all were. Tension broke out when white students began using the n-word. Clearly, some of them didn't want to be there. I felt like some of the adult white teachers didn't want to be there either. After all, this was fifteen years after the Brown v Board of Education ruling striking down segregation in 1954.

After the fourth grade, and my first encounter with white kids on a large scale, I went off to Woodruff Elementary School on the White side of the railroad tracks in 1972. The old, antiquated building greeted us bearing the name Woodruff, Founded in 1914, before WW I. There were at least three floors with creepy stairs that squeaked as one walked up and down them. It had a basement. Its walls were adorned with pictures of old bearded white guys who had taught there before. Their eyes seemed to follow me as I passed by. Behind this building were new modern classrooms that made a horseshoe facing the old building. Some of the black teachers had transferred to Woodruff, but the relationship was not the same. The principal was a young cocky white man named

Mr. Williams. He was short in stature. He was very polite and firm.

Other white teachers at Woodruff appeared courteous though clearly out of their comfort zone. Lord only knows what the experiment meant to them. My white classmates felt right at home there, but the black students were trying to get adjusted to the new environment. My performance began waning under the white teachers. I remember feeling more comfortable in the beautiful Mrs. Taylor's English class. She was black, gorgeous, and very firm as a teacher. I was starting to pay close attention to the white girls, even though we all knew not to cross any lines. Occasionally, we would play together and even walk together on our way home from school. The fifth grade went by uneventfully.

During the following summer Ocie Williams, his brother Ellis, Henry, and sisters Ruby, Alice, Alma Jean, Dorthea, Gracie, and Patricia moved to West Helena from Helena into our old house. Ocie, Ellis, and I became friends right away. Their mother Ms. Earline was an attractive stocky built woman with beautiful ebony skin. She had a warm personality, but all her children submitted to her without exception. She did not spare the rod. I began courting Alice. She had beautiful smooth ebony skin like her mother. She had bowlegs and a fine shape. Her breasts were developed, her hair was always nicely done, and she had the prettiest white teeth. She was fourteen and I was thirteen. Ocie was around eighteen, and Ellis may have been nineteen. Ellis went off to join the Army shortly after we met. They had an older brother Johnny Williams who was already in the Army. They were a very interesting family.

I began coming over to hang out with Ocie, but also to see Alice. Ocie would have all the latest records by James Brown, Al Green, Joe Tex, Jerry Butler, and other artists of that time. His mother loved Joe Simon's Drowning in the Sea of Love, and Power of Love. She also loved the latest blues songs. Occasionally, she would go out dancing with Mr. Fonzie. That gave me time to sneak around with Alice. We would sit on the back porch kissing, while Ocie would be spinning the records. Ocie introduced me to Boones Farm wine, Fighting Cock whiskey, and beer. I was smoking cigarettes already and so was he. I loved music with passion. Around this period, Al Green's I'm Still in Love was a very hot song, and Ocie had it. We would drink wine and beer until we both were tipsy. Ocie would go over to his girlfriend's house leaving me there with Alice.

Alice had the demeanor of a mature woman. Her kindness and sincerity were infectious. I'd never encountered a girl so deep. One beautiful summer afternoon, we found ourselves sitting on her bed with her smaller sisters fast asleep on the other bed. We kissed and necked until one thing led to another, and before we knew it, we were making love so passionately. When it was over we knew that this was it. We were in love. She was my girl, and I was her man whatever that meant. I had very strong feelings for her, but that didn't stop me from lusting after other attractive young ladies. Those sexual feelings were like a raging fire burning inside me at this time.

I couldn't wait to see Alice the next day, and the next one, and the next one. I was always trying to impress her. I soon learned about her previous exploits like William and Jimmy Bledsoe. Her sisters used to tease her about them. Of course, they were old news as far as I was concerned, and besides, those guys lived in Helena about 5 miles away. I was in love with Alice. She fascinated me with her walk, her smile, those beautiful white teeth, and the way she wore her hair. She could do no wrong. One day I came by. Ocie was having a drink and spinning some records, but he was not as jolly in his usual way. Alice was not in the living room, so I sat drinking with Ocie and listening to the new 45s records he had just picked up. Finally, I asked him where was Alice? He motioned his head toward her room saying she was in there. I went to her room, but the door was closed. I called out to her while opening the door at the same time. And to my surprise there she was hugged up with a bug-eyed fellow named Jimmy Bledsoe on the same bed where we had made love so passionately. I was so angry I grabbed the first thing I saw which was a clothes hanger. I threw it at her trying to knock some sense into her head. Jimmy sat there with a strange smirk on his face. Looks like Alice had not broken with her past completely. Either that, or she was just a whore. But wait a minute, wasn't I a whore too? I would have sex with any girl who would give it up at the time. I was a lady's man, just like my father, my cousin James Carter, and most of the other men in my family. So why was I so angry with Alice? Was I in love, or just in lust? Was my ego bruised or was my heart broken? I couldn't decide. But it was a terrible feeling. Who did Jim think he was, treading on my territory? Did I need to deal with this Negro physically, or deal with her?

I stayed away for a couple of days to get my thoughts together. Finally, I picked myself up off the ground and went back over to see her. I let her apologize profusely, and then I embraced her knowing all the while I was never going to see her the same way. We had been going to the field some days to make money to buy school clothes. I remember sleeping in the backyard so I wouldn't be late catching the bus at John Henry store. Alice would fry some chicken for us to have at lunch, and the aroma would have my stomach growling throughout the morning.

The first time I chopped cotton I was around eleven-years old. I would join the elders on a bus or a big field truck as we would ride down the dusty roads to a big cotton or soybean field in Cattaca Bottoms, Marvel, Arkansas, or Tunica, and Clarksdale, Mississippi just over the Mississippi River. Our chopping hoes would be stored under the bench we sat on, located on both sides of the truck bed. I would observe women wearing dresses and trousers underneath, with colorful straw hats to shield themselves from the sun. Men wore hats likewise, but I didn't get the memo. I remember wondering to myself just how long had these people been doing this work? This was 1970. But today I know that many of them had been working in those fields since the turn of the twentieth century.

Some of these field hands knew of relatives who had grappled with the evils of slavery. If we went to the field with Mr. John Henry, who owned a store, we could buy some salami, bologna, or lunch meat and some crackers for lunch. Sometimes we would buy Vienna sausages or potted meat. We could buy an ice-cold soda from Mr. John Henry once in the field. Many people brought their own lunch from home. Frugality was another trademark of the elders. We would arrive at some fields at around 6:00 A.M. while it was still cool and just at the break of dawn, and we started down those cotton or soybean rows. It was not uncommon for someone to start up a gospel song as the rhythm got going. Singing helped pass the time. Around 12:00 noon that sun was beaming on the top of our heads. The waterboys, one on each handle, were running up and across those rows with cold ice water. We all drank from the same dipper. You may let a little fall on a towel to wipe your face and neck now and then, but that sun would dry it up in no time. Ten dollars a day was a pretty sight when we got back to John Henry's store each evening, especially for a boy who didn't have many bills. I would share some of my money with my mother, but my heart's desire was to buy a pair of $10 Converse All Star tennis shoes like the big boys wore.

Alice was in sixth grade while I was in fifth grade at Woodruff. She would stop by my house so we could walk to school some mornings. We both felt like young adults who couldn't wait to leave our parents' authority and make our own decisions. Neither of us knew how important it was to finish school. School soon became a distraction. As Alice and I drifted apart, she began seeing a much older guy named Walter. He must have been around twenty. Soon Alice was pregnant. She and Walter left town to start a new life. I would see her and Walter Jr. when she came home to visit.

At this time, we lived next door to the Jones family in a house on Long Bell Street. Ms. Etta Mae was a single parent who had sons Finley Jones, Bobby, Jim, and daughters Monica, Deana, and Tracy. Ms. Etta Mae was a woman of the world. She hustled harder than any man I knew, to make sure her family was fed, clothed, and sheltered. Like all the other mothers I knew, she did not spare the rod. When she got angry about something, everybody in the house came to a halt until the problem was solved. She gambled sometimes on the line and kept a lot of money. She had a male friend that would come by. His name was Neal Bon. He was cool. I think he bought her a nice yellow Thunderbird. That was the coolest car! Her sons Bobby and Jim used to wash it, and occasionally Bobby would drive it.

Finley was the oldest. He had a big afro, and he

dressed like he came out of Hollywood. Monica, the oldest daughter, was so fine and could dance like one of the Soul Train dancers. She would blast the latest songs from the window and come outside to dance. That was my first encounter with a girl who danced so sexually suggestive. I mean she would hold me spell bound with each song. But she was much older than I. Deana became my sister's best friend, Jim became my best friend, and Bobby became my brother Jerreal's best friend. Jim was a character. We both loved music, smoked cigarettes, and drank beer. And we both chased girls. Like his momma, Jim had the filthiest mouth. And you talk about a natural comedian, that was him.

Jim and I hung out on the line at Wiley's pool hall. We'd shoot pool, play the latest songs on the jukebox, singing every word to each song. Occasionally, we would give a wino some money to go into Alp's liquor store to buy us some Boone's Farm or Golden Rod wine. We would go behind Wiley's in the alley and get tipsy. We flirted with nearly any girl that came into our space. Sometimes we went next door to Dagos and watched my cousin George Peden do the James Brown. We called him Uncle George. He was my father's first cousin. He would get drunk every weekend at Dagos and when somebody played a James Brown record on the jukebox, Uncle George would transform himself into James Brown. It was such a sight to see. He earned the nickname, James Brown. All of us were trying to be stars now that I think about it.

Maybe that was it. Jim and I wanted to be stars and we equated having a lot of girlfriends with stardom. It certainly looked that way for Elvis Presley, the Jackson 5, the Osmond Brothers and all the other hot stars on TV. Occasionally I would see a girl that was so beautiful that I said to myself, "If she would be my girl, I would never look at another one." I was grappling with an insatiable appetite to be with women, and I was trying to pinpoint the problem. Aren't I supposed to find a childhood sweetheart, fall in love, and get married when the time comes? Where did this out-of-control appetite come from anyway?

I thought about my first encounter with a female. I was five and she was our 12-year-old babysitter. She introduced us to a game called doctor and nurse. I was fascinated and looked forward to her baby sitting us again. But it never happened again; yet, my senses were completely aroused. And I stayed vigilant ready to oblige any loose girl that lured me in. Sometimes I would make the first move. But as I got older, I felt the need to work harder to get a handle on this passion. I would later turn to the church for help. But the seventies brought too much excitement and temptation. For now, I just had to play the hand that was dealt to me.

My Aunt Wadie would wake me up sometimes in the middle of the night, and say to me "Boy, you and Jim are having a time! You keep calling him a big headed motha f#@ker!" She would laugh at me. I didn't realize I was talking in my sleep. Jim and I ran together. By now I was vacillating between staying with my mother and my Aunt Pearlie on Pillow hill (Old Little Rock Road). Aunt Pearlie's house was neater than our house. When it rained, we had to put pots on the floor to catch the water due to a leaking roof. The landlord refused to keep up with repairs. But other than that, it was home.

The Brooks family lived across the street from us. They were a religious family. Rev. Ned Brooks, the father, was a friend to my stepfather Roosevelt. We played street ball with the smaller Brooks kids. I had a crush on Venise Brooks, but she was much older than me. She ended up dating my old friend Ocie Williams. Her younger sister Burdine was a young fox, but her parents were very strict, so there was no action there. She would stick her tongue out at me as if to say, "You can look, but don't touch!" If only she knew how big of a crush I had on her.

Finley Jones was that big brother that all the little brothers wanted to emulate. He was the coolest brother. Whatever Finley did Bobby, Jim, and I would try it. We even tried to walk like him. He had pretty girls, flashy clothes, stack heel shoes, and smoked reefer (Marijuana) cigarettes. He introduced us to Marijuana. I came over one day; the living room was dark with beautiful posters on the wall and a black light. The odor was strong as the smoke filled the room. Bobby passed the joint to me. War's Slipping into Darkness was on the turntable, and I was in another world. I couldn't move. The posters on the wall were glowing. Feel like I had been there for hours but in fact it had only been about forty minutes. I emerged and walked down the street with my friend Jim. I felt like I had been in some strange session which caused me to look at everything differently. I remember feeling like I was leaving my childhood and being rushed into the future, breaking with everything familiar. I was being sucked into the unknown world ahead. Soon I was normal again. I wasn't sure if I wanted to smoke any weed again or not. I liked it better in the slow pace, mundane life I was living. The weed made me hypersensitive about everything.

I got through the sixth grade at Woodruff in 1973. Bobby and Jerreal had already gone through the seventh grade at Eliza Miller Junior High School, and I was looking forward to going there. I knew there were going to be some pretty girls there from Helena and West Helena. Plus, I was becoming a big boy now. I went to school that summer, and down the hallway on bulletin boards were the names of the students and their classroom assignments. My brother told me what to expect from each teacher he knew. I was so excited. I had worked in the field and bought some nice blue jeans and shoes, so I was good to go. I immediately ran into some challenges in my Mechanical Drawing class, as well as my English class, and my reading and comprehension wasn't so fair in History and Science either.

I started getting frustrated. This stuff was over my head. My cousins Bay, David Miller, and I would meet up outside and smoke cigarettes. There would be white guys and girls there smoking also. Bay brought some white lightning to school in a small bottle, and we would skip class and drink it. This cute girl named Helen got my phone number, and started calling every night, along with another girl, Lillian. My Aunt Pearlie and cousins used to tease me about the phone calls. "Boy, them little girls got a crush on you!" they would say. One day Helen and I skipped class and walked to my house to have sex. She was a virgin, and the session ended quickly. She complained that it was too painful. So, we walked back to school. I felt I was too cool for her. I was used to more experienced girls anyhow. But we stayed friends.

Now, I was hanging out all over town in Helena at places like Kayle's night spot, Jim's Pool Hall, and Wrights Recreation Center. Kayle's, a little hole in the wall, was jumping every weekend. All the latest Soul Train Jams and dances were happening there. Central High School students and adults alike were jumping in that place. The Bloodstone's Natural High was the song to slow drag to, that's when you dance close to the girl so that your private parts meet through your clothes. I think most of the guys in there had the same thing on their minds - sex. Sometimes I would leave the club with a much older woman and spend time at her house before hitchhiking back to West Helena later that night. Someone was always headed back and forth from Helena to West Helena. And the people were so courteous and friendly. Sometimes Jim and I would hop on the back of a truck or pile into the back seat of a car. They would drop us off on the line and we would walk home. This was our routine most weekends.

It was around this time that I was at Kayle's one Friday and a beautiful white Duce and a Quarter pulled up. I heard someone call me, "Sputnik!" The window rolled down and I saw that it was my cousin Charles Suggs with another cousin, Ellis riding shotgun. But where did he get the money to buy a ride like that, I wondered. I hopped into the back seat. It had a black leather interior and a smooth sounding eight-track. They were listening to Al Green's Call Me album and man did it sound good. They were smoking a joint which they passed back to me. Before I knew it, I was listening intently to the words of Green's Jesus is Waiting and Stand Up! We rode down to Helena Crossing and pulled up to a juke joint, where we saw Ruby, a new classmate of mine at Eliza Miller. She had a crush on Charles, and when we got back to school that's all she could talk about. She would ask me if we were coming back to the juke joint this Friday.

I kind of felt important riding around with my cousin. That car was turning heads. I was starting to pay more attention to cars then, mainly for how they attracted women. The weekend rolled around again, and I was looking forward to seeing that clean, white, ride coming around the corner. Once, Jim was with me, and we both jumped into the back seat. We rode around smoking weed and sipping on Strawberry Hill

Boones Farm. When Charles dropped us back off at Kayle's, Jim got out looking at the ride as if to say, "Man, that's some ride!" It was 1973, and it seems everybody was having a blast!

White kids in Helena-West Helena enjoyed riding up and down Cherry Street on weekends, a block over from Kayle's Night Spot. Our worlds never connected. But we all were celebrating life. The American Band Stand was to young whites what Soul Train was to young blacks, although I loved watching both music shows. I loved music, and the excitement it brought to all people. I was listening to Elton John's Bennie and the Jets, Paul McCartney's Band on the Run, the Story's Louie, Louie, the Doobie Brothers, and Dr. Hooks. For me, music said that there was no black or white. Only a human being with a soul could produce such melodic sounds, and lyrics that portrayed my deepest feelings, and so it was with music by the Carpenters, John Denver, and Barry Manilow, as well as all the black artists I listened to.

I need to say something about our yearnings to be recognized for some achievement. I used to hear a term used by the elders "he/she is a credit to her/his race." They would say this about Jackie Robinson, Willie Mays, or Fannie Lou Hamer, etc. I'm not sure if white people started using the phrase or black people. Abraham Maslow came up with the theory of Pyramids of Needs in 1943, one of which had to do with self-esteem. This theory could have been at work, or the aftermath of slavery led to a natural competitiveness in a climate where blacks were considered inferior. The bar for us was set high by local and national black achievers. I always sought the praise and approval of the elders. But with my peers, there was a new kind of challenge. My friend Bobby and Jimmy boasted about traveling to Caruthersville, Missouri to visit their grandmother for the summer. Sometimes we encountered friends in the neighborhood who had been to Chicago or Detroit. My siblings and I had never left town. We felt like backward, country boys, uncouth. Finley Jones would go away and come back wearing the most fashionable threads from hats to shoes. Every now and then Bobby and Jimmy would get new threads, and they would come outside to show them off. Jim had a habit of walking down the street with a dap in his walk looking at his shoes as he went. I too would do that when I dressed up.

We all took great care of our afros like the Jacksons, or the dancers on Soul Train. This was the style. Everything we did seemed like it was for attention, especially female attention. I needed to add travel to my credentials. If I could boast to the ladies that I had visited certain large cities, I would surely be even more popular like Finley Jones. But I feared living in cities like St. Louis or Chicago after hearing different friends talk about their encounters with gang members and bullies of all sorts.

West Helena was civilized, I thought, compared to those places. I didn't realize that there were bad parts of these cities and good parts. My father had traveled throughout the country. He spoke about good experiences and bad. I just wanted to bolster my reputation. Bragging was a big part of our youth here in West Helena. Sometimes we made up stories about where we had been, or what our big brothers had done. Perhaps it was due to low self-esteem. Most of my friends needed to have their egos stroked. And I still see it in people to this day.

Playing the dozens was a big part of our lives at this time also. This meant roasting each other from time to time. Jim and I could be walking down the street and encounter his brother Bobby in the company of other friends, and one of them might say "looka here! Ole big headed-ass Jim and that Chinese looking-ass Sputnik!" "Where y'all taking y'all's raggedy asses to?" Everybody would crack up laughing. Jim might say something like "That's alright! Your momma likes it!" One had to be very careful with those momma jokes. That could end the dozens and lead right into a serious fist fight. You had to know your opponent.

Kenny Price stuttered, and that alone would have us rolling on the ground, but he was so good at playing the dozens that he would have us laughing at ourselves. I believe that if he had gone into comedy, America would never be the same. I could say that about locals, such as Willie Robinson, Nathan Robinson, and Jim. They were natural. As I think about it, I knew some of the greatest athletes that ever played the games. Self-doubt, a lack of opportunities, and sometimes a stacked deck, kept them from making it. There's a lot of truth in Sly and the Family Stone's song "Everybody is a Star."

The West Helena 4

Somewhere around the middle of the school year at Eliza Miller in 1974, I met this little guy named Michael Bowman. He was a chubby young fellow about twelve years old. He had a round face, wide nose, with dark rings around his nose and eyes. We exchanged names. I told him my name was Sputnik. He laughed and said "Smut-nick!" I thought he was making fun of my name, but that was the kind of guy he was. He was good-natured and funny. He said he had come from Detroit, Michigan to go to school, because he got into trouble back there. He lived with his sister Lisa, and his mother Ms. Wilma Bowman near Eliza Miller in an area called New Addition. We walked home from school daily.

Sometimes Mike and I would play basketball in the neighborhood or go up to West Gibson shopping store where his mom worked. Occasionally, Michael would have a wad of cash. I asked him where he had gotten this money. He said, "I know how to shortchange people." Well, he was from Detroit, that was a city of gangsters to me. I didn't care to learn any illegal methods for getting money. We chopped cotton in summer or mowed lawns. I explained to him that I got my money the old fashion way. But Michael was cool! He didn't smoke cigarettes, and he didn't drink.

Once I convinced Mike to buy me $5 worth of weed that came in a small brown envelope called a nickel bag. He walked with me over to my Aunt Pearlie's house. I fired up a joint and passed it to him, but he frowned and waved me away. It was getting late in the evening as we arrived at my aunt's house. I was going to tell her that I was spending the night at Michael's house. On our way back we walked past this white church on a hill across the street from Aunt Pearlie's. And we both heard this weird sound. Michael paused, and said to me "Smut-nick, did you hear that?" Well, I had smoked a joint, but I too was hearing the same scary noise. Michael took off running, and I joined him. It was a sight to see how that little fat boy ran. We made it to the residential area on Lambert Drive and laughed till our stomachs were sore. I knew I wasn't going to pass that church at night anymore. I learned later that some prisoners may have escaped and took up residence at the church. But it became a haunted church to me.

We arrived at Michael's house, and his mother wore beautiful evening attire as if she was going out. She was very beautiful and very friendly. She played music on her turntable, as Michael and I raided her kitchen. Lisa and Michael would have their sibling spats, or they would tease each other about something. Michael and I had much to talk about, teachers at school, a basketball game, or running past that scary white church. That night when the house was settled, and Michael was sleeping, I would lay there listening to the entire For the Good Times album by Al Green. Was Ms. Bowman missing someone back in Detroit, maybe her children's father, or some previous lover? I didn't know, but I loved her taste in music. I looked forward to going by and spending the night occasionally. My brother Jerreal had dropped out of school and enlisted into the Job Corp. Other guys our age was doing the same. I thought about doing it. We received pictures and letters my brother sent us from the Cass Conservation Center in Ozark, Arkansas. My brother said he was learning a trade, and that there were other guys there from West Helena.

I always looked up to my big brother. He was the curly head one. He was tall, lanky, and quiet. I always tried to stay on his good side growing up, but every now and then we would get into a fight. It wouldn't last long though. I remember an incident where we were at a baseball game getting ready to play. Team members were being selected, and there was this bully there named Vincent Brown. He and I had crossed paths a couple of times and got into wrestling matches.

Vincent would out best me every time. But on this day, he came up to me to start a fight, and his big brother was edging him on. Before I knew it, I was in a headlock and on the ground. I was swinging, but my blows meant nothing. His brother was saying "kill that nigger, Vincent!" The next thing I knew, Jerreal had come over and started throwing blows, and he got Vincent in a headlock. His brother tried to intervene, but a big fierce football player named Bailey House looked at him and said, "You better not touch him!"

Bailey House was one of the baddest brothers on the block. There's an old saying, if you see him and a bear fighting, help the bear. My brother not only showed courage that day, but he also revealed a deeper love for his little brother I had never seen.

I missed that curly headed boy. I told my mother that I would like to drop out of school and go where he was. Mother was not in favor of such a move, so I continued at Eliza Miller. My grades were not improving, and it was becoming increasingly frustrating. I couldn't understand why the other students were getting it, but I couldn't. One day I was sitting in Ms. Osborne's music class in the back of the room making my fellow classmates laugh.

Music is the subject that I should have tried the hardest to learn. Instead, I was interrupting the class. Ms. Osborne scolded me and asked me to stop. She was a slim, blonde, Caucasian woman with a seemingly mean temper. I stopped but started up again. "Joseph Wheeler!" she screamed. "Get out into the hallway!" Everybody knew that meant she was going to paddle me with her wooden board. She went across the hall to get another teacher to witness the punishment. My ego was bruised, and I said to her point blank "You are not paddling me." She said "Fine! Go to the office!" I walked into the principal's office, and Mr. Williams said to me "So you like to disrupt the class. Bend over and grab that desk!" I told him "I'm not taking a paddle today." He said, "Is that so?" He sat down and began to write out a suspension slip. He looked up and handed me the slip and said "Give this to your parents. You have been suspended for the rest of the year." As I let those heavy double doors close behind me I knew I had screwed up big time. If only I could see the trouble I would face in the future. I was mostly staying with Aunt Pearlie during this time. I went there and told her what had happened. Aunt Pearlie was infuriated. I never wanted to let her or Momma down. Aunt Pearlie said "You took your little smart ass to that school and started running your mouth, now what your little ass gone do? You are too young to get a job." I told her I might join the Job Corps like Jerreal. She didn't want to hear it. I had never seen her so angry. Momma took it all in stride. She said, "I guess you will have to join the Job Corps!" Mother had only made it to the sixth grade. Aunt Pearlie dropped out too, but they wanted their children to do better. I felt awful.

I still had a chance to sign up for the federal government's CETA job program and make summer money, so I went to the school and applied. Mr. Sherman Sims was the coordinator who came around and assigned us to teams to cut grass along the side of the roads and in the city parks. Sherman had a shiny, apple green, 442 Buick. And man was that car sharp! We were to start a week after school let out for the summer. I was excited to make my first paycheck with my name on it. I believe school let out on that Friday, May 22, 1974. For all the school kids this was a time for celebration. No more school for a while. We could play if we wanted without having to worry about getting up for school the next morning.

I had already been out for a few weeks. Normally, Jim and I would get together and go up to Wiley's to shoot pool, or hitchhike over to Helena to meet girls and dance at Kale's. But this Friday, I was at Aunt Pearlie's playing with 9-month-old Andria, my cousin Marilyn's daughter. I bounced her on my knee and played patty cakes with her. She laughed until she fell asleep on my chest. I got up and put her to bed. By then the sun was going down. I was not going to walk by that spooky church, and all my cousins knew about my fear of that church. I was in for the night.

I had a rule, If I couldn't make it to Aunt Pearlie's house before dark, I would stay at my mother's house and vice versa. I must have gone to bed around ten o'clock that Friday night. It was unusual for me to be home on Friday, much less going to bed that early. The next morning, I heard grown folks talking in the living room, and it sounded urgent. Someone came into my room and said "Sputnik, the police need to see you." What was this about? I thought, wiping the sleep from my eyes. I walked down the hall to the living room to find West Helena Police Chief Earl Gilcrest and Aunt Pearlie looking at me. Chief Gilcrest said "Boy you're supposed to be dead!" as he waved a piece of paper with a list of names on it. "Come and go with me. I need you to identify some boys for me." I got dressed and got into the backseat of the police sedan. Jimmy Hunter was already in the backseat. I asked him "What's going on, man?" He said he didn't know either. We rode along quietly, hearing only the dispatcher and officers on the police radio. Soon we arrived at Jackson Highley Funeral parlor. We followed the chief up this long flight of stairs. He opened the door and motioned us to come in. Nothing could have prepared me for the gruesome scene I was about to witness. There lying on mattresses were four mangled bodies with knots on their heads, and gashes of meat that had been torn from their limbs. I immediately recognized Michael Bowman, with his arm completely severed from his body and lying between his legs. His face looked like a rubber Halloween mask, so disfigured; yet, I could see the black rings around his nose and eyes. I recognized Johnny Lee, Robert Hayes, and Jimmy recognized Eddie Jackson.

Rumors had it that the boys were coming back home from Walnut Corner on Hwy 49 and decided to lie down in the middle of the highway, and an eighteen-wheeler hit them. I couldn't imagine Michael doing something like that. Later we heard that someone had placed them in a large box and placed the box on the highway. Even that sounded a bit bizarre. Soon, people began saying that there were two boys with them and got away, and one of them was Sputnik. Some of my friends began pointing their fingers at me saying you know something but not telling us.

I couldn't believe how a rumor could take on a life of its own. I went to see Michael's mother to tell her how sorry I was about the loss of her son. She pulled me aside at West Gibson and began interrogating me asking me to tell her what I knew. I tried to explain to her that I was not with her son Friday night. She did not believe me. I can hear the pain in her voice to this day. God only knows what agony the other parents must have gone through. I had seen the sixteen-year-old Johnny Lee riding his bicycle up and down the streets of West Helena numerous times. He was close friends with Jerreal Lee. I went to school with Robert Hayes and his sister Emma. I saw Eddie and his family members before. In West Helena on the black side of town you would cross paths with each other somewhere, and you would know their faces even if you didn't know their names. People were asking for me by my street name, and they were white people. I was feeling uncomfortable about that. They could have been white investigators, but what if they were not? What if they were associates of the killer(s)?

I was on edge. A week later I started working on my CETA job cutting grass in the white city park near 10th Street. My friends Bobby Jones, Kenney Price, and Timothy Carter began taunting me saying, "Sputnik, you ought to say something. They say you were with them boys." I kept refuting those rumors, but no one was convinced except momma, my Aunt Pearlie, and her children. I believe the rumor started because Jimmy and I identified the bodies. It didn't help that my name was on the list Chief Gilcrest had either. One day I was cutting grass and one of my friends said his mother overheard some white folks asking for me by name at the Fish Market. He said, "They gone try to kill you next." What if it was true? I thought. This killer(s) was ruthless, and it seemed that the police were doing nothing to find him or them.

Job Corps

I went to my mother and told her that I feared for my life, and that I needed to get in touch with relatives in Chicago so I could go there and stay until this thing blew over. Mother didn't have any money for the bus fare. She suggested that I go and see Mr. Wiley, the owner of Wiley's Pool Hall. I think he was a military veteran who worked at the Department of Labor office in Helena. He was the one who helped my brother get into Job Corp. I met with him and completed the application. Mr. Wiley had to raise my age, because one had to be at least sixteen to join. I was fifteen. I was given a departure date after I left the office. Running away from a problem that was too big for me to solve felt wrong in a way. But if the adults couldn't bring about justice, who was I?

I realized that I wasn't ready to leave my mother and all that was so familiar to me. But what would happen if I stayed? My departure day came. Mr. Wiley gave me a Continental Trailway bus ticket to San Marcos, Texas. Wait a minute! This must have been a mistake, I thought. I was trying to go to the Cass Conservation Center in Ozark, Arkansas where my brother was. I tried to reach Mr. Wiley so he could change the paperwork. I finally tracked him down, but he told me that Cass was all filled up. I was put on the bus. I remember crying as I watched my little town disappear.

I rode up Hwy 49 past where the West Helena 4 were found in the road. We went down Route 1 across the St. Francis River and continued on to Interstate 40 through Memphis. I had never been that far from home in my life. I had heard my friends bragging about visiting Chicago, St. Louis, Detroit, and other major cities, but I was going to Texas. We changed buses in Texarkana. I walked around the terminal carrying my brown paper bag with a shirt and a pair of pants. The voice on the intercom said "*Now boarding passengers in lane 7 for Dallas, Waco-Ft. Worth, Austin, San Marcos, etc.*" I jumped up and walked briskly out the door to my bus. It was dark when we reached Dallas, but I was impressed with the tall buildings, expressways, and city lights for miles. I arrived at my destination at night.

On June 26, 1974, I enlisted into the Gary Job Corps Center in San Marcos, Texas. It was a hot Texas Summer. After completing orientation and moving to what was called the blocks (each dorm was named blue block, red block, brown block etc.) I ran into my cousin El Freeman, along with other guys from my neck of the woods. We met up at the swimming pool. I was not a swimmer; in fact, I was terrified of deep water. I stayed in the five feet range and flopped around. Other guys were playing and jumping into the eight feet section. I got out and walked around the pool and before I knew it, El pushed me into the eight feet of water. There I was fighting the water fearing that I would drown for sure. I managed to hold my breath and somehow make it to the five feet section.

El and I nearly came to blows that day. But I learned something about swimming. There would be many other lessons that I would learn that way, not because I wanted to, but because I had to. Fear is a very tricky thing. It can stop you from reaching your full potential if you let it.

I came into the Job Corps plagued with a bladder control problem. Bed wetting had been a nagging, persistent, problem since I was a small child. Beatings and shaming did nothing to resolve my issue. But in Job Corps I was facing raw peer pressure. Although I was 15, I had declared myself a man. I had to earn respect from the other guys, none of whom had a problem with bed wetting. I would stay up late running back and forth to the bathroom. Around 4 a.m. I would fall asleep only to be awakened by the dorm advisor around 6 a.m. I was elated to see that my underwear was dry. This went on for about 2 weeks. By the time I reached the blocks I was completely cured from bed wetting. My confidence received a big lift.

Now, if only my attention-deficit could improve. Sitting in the classroom was still a challenge for me. My mind would be all over the place. I couldn't focus on one thing. The teachers tried their best to teach me, but not with the mandate that the race teachers had during my school segregation years. I was in the classroom physically, but not mentally; however, I was fully involved in my vocation of meat cutting. I did very well and was able to land a job with Food City

Supermarket in San Antonio upon completion in 1975. I would have difficulty finding another well-paying job without a GED once I lost my first job. I truly resented not being able to focus and comprehend English, math, science, history, and literature. After dropping out of Eliza Miller Junior High school in the seventh grade,

I wanted nothing more than to finish high school. But between marijuana, partying, and chasing girls, I lacked the discipline, and the attention span to achieve it. It never occurred to me at the time that the school curriculum was not set up for black children to achieve. It was certainly not designed for us to arrive at some sense of autonomy. At best we could be prepared to receive a benevolent position somewhere in a company. For example, history was not told from the experience we endured. Therefore, it was rather boring, exclusively white. All my life I had been surrounded by streets named for early explorers and Confederate heroes like Desoto, Lasalle, Cleburne, and Jefferson Davis. I had no interest in investigating these people. I saw Confederate statues, and a prominent statue of a Doughboy in Helena, but these statues served to spark pride in white people, and to affirm their superiority. Few symbols reflected the footprint of the Indigenous people; a river, street name, or a tobacco product with a chief's head on it was the most I saw. I didn't know that a part of their story was imbedded in my own family history.

At the time that I signed up for Job Corps I knew

very little about the program. My brother, Jerreal had dropped out of school in 1974, and enrolled into the Job Corps at the Cass Conservation Center in Ozark, Arkansas. He would write letters home with pictures of him and other guys from West Helena. It seemed like a pretty cool place. Unbeknownst to both of us at the time, Job Corps had been instituted during Lyndon B. Johnson's Administration in 1964 as a part of his "War on Poverty" strategy. He sought to enhance economic and social opportunities for the poor, especially minorities. This was one of his Great Society initiatives. Both of my meat cutting instructors, Joe Quiroz, a Hispanic, and Joe Scott, a Caucasian, were military veterans. In fact, Gary Job Corps Center had been established in 1965 on a WW II Air Force training base. And that's exactly what it looked like in 1974 when I arrived.

We were told that Heavyweight Boxing Champion, George Forman got his start at that site. There were thousands of young men there from around the country and territories like Puerto Rico, and the US Virgin Island. I even met Cubans and Jamaican brothers there. There were few whites. Gary Job Corps had three major cafeterias that provided us three square meals a day. I didn't get three square meals back home. There, we got a physical, and we saw a dentist. We were issued Job Corps uniforms with name tags and black shoes and half boots which we wore daily while in training. We were assigned details cleaning windows, buffing floors, mowing the lawns, etc., just like in the military.

The old WW II barracks had cranks to open the windows. If you enter the elongated building on the right side, you will walk down a long corridor passing rooms we called cubicles on the right and the latrine/showers on the left. As you came to another division there were two more cubicles on the right and finally you reached the end where there was a bunk straight ahead and a cubicle to the right of it. When you went out you passed another exit door opposite the cubicles. We took turns buffing that long corridor as well as our own rooms. Our beds had to be made up daily military style. I learned a degree of discipline while I was there.

But during recreation time some of us guys would sit around smoking weed and listening to the latest soul music. The O'Jay's *Ship Ahoy* album was hot at the time. A Jamaican dude named Foy was playing the Four Tops and all the Motown sounds. I met up with a guy named Garrett from North Philly. He was into cool caps, and easy walker shoes. He introduced me to the sounds of Santana. *That Black Majic Woman* album was happening especially when I was under the influence of weed. During my early days in the program, I kept seeing these people with long dark black hair, they were brown people. I thought they were Indians. One day we were sitting around "token weed" as we called it, and one of these brown guys came around. After getting high I looked at him and asked him his name. He said his name was Mike Sanchez. I asked him if he was an Indian. Everyone started laughing at me. Mike said "Nah, I'm a f#*cking

Mexican, a Chicano man!" He passed the joint my way, as he proceeded to teach me some of the bad words in Spanish. We arose from there, and he asked me if I was hungry. This was after 7:00 p.m. The cafeteria was long closed. I said yeah, but where would we find food? I followed him down to the back of the cafeteria where there was a big walk-in freezer. He broke into it and started handing me apples and oranges. We creeped out and ran back to the barracks watching out for the brown cars that the security guards drove. He was laughing like it was no big deal. I was worried about getting kicked out of the program.

I continued getting high with Mike and learning Spanish words to try on the momasitas in town, but I didn't go on anymore food excursions with him. My friend Garrett had a dark side also. He used to tell me about his friends back in Philly, and how they used to rob people. One day following payday (we would get $15 dollars a month) he and a friend decided to rob the Job Corps bank that was housed in a wood frame storage-like building. They got caught. I watched the security officers lead him out of the barracks in handcuffs. I'm not sure about what happened to him. Some say he went to prison. He was such a bright kid. There were a lot of bright young men in Job Corp, and many of them went on to have great careers.

I went to church occasionally. There was always some religious zealot going around trying to convert Job Corpsmen. We had at least two post chapels, one for Catholics, and one for Protestants. I went to the latter, not that I understood the different traditions. The Catholic church was too liturgical and structured, whereas the protestant church was more free style. There was a fire baptized Mexican preacher at the church who had a beautiful daughter about a year younger than me. She had the cutest smile. I'm not sure who held my attention the most, the preacher or his daughter. Pastor Debrail preached under the anointing, and at times it seems he was speaking directly to me.

I was starting to read the scriptures more these days. I think this pastor pricked my conscience about hell and condemnation for sin. I was young and wild. Getting high, listening to soul music, and chasing girls was what I lived for. There were no girls on post, just a few foxy teachers and dorm advisors. Other than that, there were guys who wanted to be girls. Now that was something I wasn't used to. I remember one drag queen in Helena who went by the name of Major. He was a full figured bright-skinned man who dressed up like a woman. Most weekends he would frequent the nightclubs. My friend Jim and I used to get a good laugh watching him. One day Jim called out to Major saying *"Major, ya big fat fagoty mutha f#%ker!"* Major pulled a 38 revolver out of his purse, and Jim and I hauled our asses. That was the end of our mocking gay people. There was one other time I was drinking with an older guy, Peaches, in Helena in 1974. We started out walking down an alley way and Peaches spotted a slender light-skinned brother dressed in a fancy burgundy cashmere Maxey coat.

That was a sharp coat. Peaches whispered to me saying *"this guy is a fag. Come on I'm gonna get some money."* Peaches began hitting the lad. He took his coat and gave it to me. The brother didn't put up a defense. I told Peaches to leave him alone. We left him on one knee holding his face. I hitchhiked back to West Helena with the man's coat. I felt so guilty. For days I had the coat at my house, but I was afraid to wear it; moreover, my conscience wouldn't let me rest. I went back to Helena the following weekend hoping to find the owner. But I never saw him again. I resolved in my mind not to ever harm or let anyone talk me into harming another human being again, gay or straight.

With that being said, I encountered some gay men at Gary Job Corps and later in San Antonio where I went to party every weekend. Some gay guys at Gary would make one do a double take. I got a chance to talk to some of them about their lives, and what made them live that lifestyle. Each one had a different story. One was molested as a child. Another one had been incarcerated and changed while in jail. Still others said it was their preference. All I knew is that I had not found anything better than a woman. So, I concluded, to each his own.

I couldn't wait to get to San Antonio. From time to time, we would go to Austin, Texas on Tuesdays. Most of the Corpsmen went to the clubs on 12th Street, but that's where all the drag queens hung out. You would be lucky to find two or three real girls there with the drags. I went there for beer, and to hear some music always hoping to get lucky and find a real girl. Sometimes I would visit a fair close to downtown Austin and try to hit on the few black girls milling around or try out my weak Spanish on the Mexican girls. At best I would make them laugh. White girls were not off limits either. Austin was always a letdown.

I credit my faith in God for keeping me from going to the extreme about sex, drugs, fame, money etc. I remember feeling sorry for the gay men who seemingly had no guardrails. Many of them were proud of the life they chose. Yet, I met one or two who attended church with me trying to arrest those demons fighting from within. For them it was inordinate affection for members of the same sex, while for me it was an insatiable appetite for the opposite sex. The preacher at Gary gave powerful sermons on the deceit of fornication. He warned us of the hell fire that awaited all fornicators. I was convinced on the one hand and on the other hand, I was lusting after his fourteen-year-old daughter. She was so young, beautiful, and innocent. But I had been out into the world where I had been exposed to grown up things. Perhaps it was for that reason I could understand the scriptures. I had engaged in many of the things the scriptures spoke against. Some of the scripture was like looking in the mirror at myself and questioning the sanity of my lustful passion.

My conscience was impacted by religion as early as the time I was four. Living two doors down from Ms. Annie Miles afforded me opportunities to talk to her about God. She had a big picture of a white, blond haired, blue-eyed, Jesus walking on the water. She explained that picture as best she could. The image of this figure walking on the water stayed with me for years. I have since dismissed this white depiction of a Palestinian Jew named Jesus. It corresponded to an account in the Bible sprinkled with a little white supremacy. I would see mother praying often after she had come home from Little Rock. She described the institution as a dreadful place, and she always feared going back there. The experience was so horrible that she didn't want to visit a doctor now for anything. She thought they would find another spot on her lungs and admit her once again. So, prayer was her secret weapon. She would get sick often. Sometimes she caught a bad cold from cutting wood in the sleet and snow.

My brother and I didn't want to think about parting with Momma again. It seemed that her prayers were working. And when she started taking us to church regularly, I saw a marked improvement in our quality of life. Jerreal and I even got baptized in a muddy lake at Lakeview, Arkansas and started attending Wofford Chapel Baptist church off Old Little Rock Road around 1973. It happened to be that I would feel empty if I didn't attend church on Sunday no matter how devilish I had been during the week. I was striving to be a good person. Church was foundational. Little did I realize at the time, I was learning more about the Christian faith by watching and interacting with other Christians, but I knew very little about how Christianity was appropriated by those who enslaved my ancestors. I knew nothing about the role Christianity played in the colonization of Africa and the exploitation of other people.

San Antonio

San Antonio was the town! Any given Saturday around 1:20 P.M. our blue Job Corps bus would pull up beside a tin beige building next to the railroad tracks and a stone's throw from the famous Freeman Coliseum on E. Houston Street on the Eastside of town. Inside the lounge one could sit in an air-conditioned space and play pool. We would walk or take the transit downtown. San Antonio was bustling with people shopping or site seeing. There were fresh Lackland Air Force recruits dressed in their dark blue service uniforms, tourists taking pictures around the Alamo, or conventioneers at the Hemisphere Convention Center. There were girls everywhere.

My afro was shining from the Afro Sheen I sprayed on before I left Gary. I was wearing my stack heel shoes, bell bottom jeans, and a colorful shirt. My eyes caught this beautiful 15-year-old named Vicky. I laid my rap down. She told me that she was a foster kid who lived on the East Side. We walked down to the River Walk and sat on a bench and talked further. I kissed her before we parted and made plans to meet her again the following weekend at the same place. I couldn't wait. Saturday rolled around, but she was a no show. Then I met a beautiful, slender built, hazel-eyed cutie named Kimberly Evans. We walked around downtown. She and her sister Gee Gee convinced me and a couple of my friends to take the bus to their house out in Denver Heights on the East Side. We hung out until It was time to go back to the Job Corps Lounge and ride back to Gary. After a sweet kiss, we agreed to get together the next weekend. There was going to be a battle of the bands live music festival in Pittman Sullivan Park. That was right up my alley because music was my thing.

The following weekend was phenomenal! My friends and I had bought brand new clothes to wear to the event. It was a beautiful evening. I wore mint green bell bottoms and a flashy dark green and White pullover with stack heel shoes. Kimberly and her friends brought a blanket to lay out on the grass. Soon the park was full. Guys from the neighborhood dressed like the Jacksons, kind of bourgeois. Many of the girls wore tight daisy dukes. I was like a kid in a candy store, trying to give Kim my undivided attention. The music started and the whole park was caught up in the groove. The bands played all the latest songs of the time. Kim and her friends got up to dance. We joined in. Marijuana fumes were in the air. I looked closely at a brother dressed in a green shirt with Air Force designs and a dark blue cap. It was my cousin Bruce Braiden from West Helena. He was in training at Lackland Air Force base. We had some small talk and got back to the mission at hand which was admiring all the beautiful women there. Talk about a small world. I was learning just how small it was.

The following Saturday, we went back downtown San Antonio. This time Vicky showed up. We went down to the river walk and sat on a bench with a view of the passers-byes on the bridge. As we sat down, my eyes caught a glimpse of Gee Gee pulling Kim's arm telling her to look at the two-timer sitting on the bench cheating on her. She looked at me and walked away in anger. I ran up the stairs and down the sidewalk to catch up to her. But she wasn't interested in anything I had to say. Gee Gee gave me this disgusting look. I spoke to Kim on the phone a few times after that, but things would never be the same. I was conflicted. This relationship thing was a piece of work. Kim wanted complete loyalty. I just wanted to have a good time. Still, in the back of my mind, I knew I would feel the same way had the shoe been on the other foot.

I convinced myself to stop taking these relationships so seriously. Afterall, I was only fifteen and certainly not yet ready for marriage. Soon I started hanging out at Poppy Lounge, a hot little hole in the wall next door to the Job Corps Lounge on E. Houston Street. Older women went there along with drag queens and other gay men. I met Karen, Deborah, and her sister Nancy there. They smoked weed and didn't mind passing the joint. I went home with Karen and a few of her friends one Saturday night. We puffed and drank beer into the night. She knew what I wanted most, and she gradually led me there. I woke up the next morning ready for round two.

My appetite was insatiable. Karen was around twenty-two, and I was fifteen going on thirty. She and her friends dropped me off at the Job Corp Lounge that Sunday after breakfast. I had to mill around until 10 o'clock P.M. because that's when the bus would arrive to take us back to Job Corps. There wasn't much to do on a Sunday afternoon, but I saw two cute young ladies going to a local convenient store. I caught up to them. They were giggling, I learned they had just smoked a joint. Katie was a light-skinned sister with a beautiful, short, cropped afro. She had these beautiful hazel eyes. Her friend was equally beautiful. Michelle had straightened hair with two pigtails. She had beautiful ebony skin. It was hard to choose, but Katie was strong-willed and confident. She knew what she wanted, and it was not me. But we became the best of friends. In fact, in a year and a half, she would be the one to come to my rescue.

East Terrace Projects and Vanessa

Poppy Lounge attracted folks from the East Terrace
Housing Projects, also. Jeanette was around twenty-
five, a little on the thick side. This dark-skinned sister
wore eyeglasses, and she acted like a strict chaperone
as she led Shirley, Vanessa, and Chi Chi down the
railroad tracks to the Job Corp Lounge and Poppy
Lounge. Come to find out, Jeanette had married a
former Job Corpsmen herself. I started flirting with
Vanessa. The following weekend a Corpsmen named
Jessie and I walked the railroad tracks down to the
East Terrace. We noticed out on the basketball court
young people had started to gather to dance. The DJ
was playing the latest sounds like Do the Hustle. This
song had the guys and girls lined up in a formation,
and it was exciting to see them dance with so much
style and precision.

Later, the DJ played the Ohio Players' hit, Fire, the
very song that Vanessa and I danced to the prior
weekend at Poppy's. My eyes caught sight of who I
thought was Vanessa. This short beautiful ebony girl
was getting down. When the song was over, I went to
ask her if she remembered me from last weekend. She
told me "No!" I accused her of having selective
amnesia now that she was around her friends. She
countered "You must be talking about my sister
Vanessa." I said "Yes! That's huh name, Vanessa.
Where is she?" She went to get her, and they both
came down to the court. I had mistaken Mary Lee for

Vanessa. This is how our friendship began. I was able to get Vanessa's older sister, Betty Ann, to write out a sponsorship letter to the Job Corp allowing me to spend the weekend at her apartment from Friday until Sunday night. Vanessa lived with her mother, father, sister and four brothers upstairs from Betty Ann.

According to the housing agreement, no men were supposed to be living in the apartments. They could only visit. While no one adhered to that rule, it did give men excuses to come and go as they pleased. Vanessa's father, Mr. Felton Franks Sr., lived with her mother, although loosely. Betty Ann was shacking up (staying together but not married) with her baby's father Michael. And there were similar arrangements throughout the projects. We used to sit around at Betty's smoking weed and drinking as we listened to music. Betty cooked wonderful Spanish dishes that I enjoyed so much. I ventured out and got to know other people living in this large housing project. Mostly, I was treated with warm hospitality. Occasionally tension arose between the Job Corp boys and the local guys who were suspicious of us dating their women. There was a time when a corpsman, Arnold Jones from Houston, got into a fight with a local.

Arnold, who resembled the actor Richard Roundtree, was dating Vanessa's friend Lenora. Apparently, he had made some kind of promise to this drag queen named Bae Bae and the latter confronted him. Blows started passing, and Bae Bae drew a knife.

111

Before long the whole project, it seemed, had come to see the fight and edge Bae Bae on. A gun was pulled, and everyone scattered. I heard "Let's get them Job Corps niggers!" Arnold, Jessie, I, and other Job Corpsmen took to the railroad tracks, and we didn't look back. We heard people running after us hurling insults. We managed to get to the Job Corp Lounge. After the commotion subsided, I walked over to Katie's house nearby and stayed there until it was time for the bus to leave.

Those were my first lessons about project life, and I would learn many more. At the time, I was not familiar with the history of the housing project. I'm sure few of the tenants knew the history either. Most were on welfare, but like me they were doing something to better their lives. Also like me, some had dropped out of school and could not access jobs paying decent wages. Although some of the men had jobs, others had consigned themselves to a life of crime, and hustling. Still, I met others who were taking classes in nursing, cosmetology, and other endeavors.

The housing program followed the great depression (1933) and was initially started to help the poor find temporary housing until they could be integrated into regular housing. But in essence it became a tool for segregation. By the 1960s and 70s these projects were all over the country. It wasn't long before people of the middle and upper class began moving away from these centers for fear that their property value would plummet, or they would become a victim of a crime. In hindsight, I can clearly see how the housing rules did little to promote family unity. It essentially penalized the woman for allowing the male to live in the home. If both adults were working and had a plan for upward mobility, they needed the necessities of life to help them reach their goals. Housing was the greatest need. I experienced this firsthand as did some of my friends.

Public Housing

I had wonderful experiences living in the East Terrace. I met wonderful people there and some are still friends of mine. I witnessed the daily struggles of single mothers and young men like me. I listened to them express their dreams and aspirations to me. Most of all, I heard the stories of the elders and how they ended up in public housing. Mr. and Mrs. Franks had moved to San Antonio from Flatonia, Texas sometime during the 60s. They had been involved in fieldwork in Flatonia with little chance of improving their quality of life. In San Antonio, Mr. Franks, and his brother Tommy D. found better employment with which to sustain their families. To their children they stressed the importance of education just as the elders back home did to us. But according to some politicians, people on welfare were content with receiving government handouts. Nothing could be farther from the truth than this myth. Poor people want what others want.

As a child in West Helena, I was always drawn to the elders. I learned so much from them and some would say I had an old soul in a fifteen-year-old's body. It seemed that people my age had very little to teach me. Besides, I felt appreciated and affirmed by the elders, and all the young people who saw their affection for me knew not to mistreat me. I talked religion with them, and I let them know my goals, and why I was in Job Corps. They praised me and encouraged me to continue. I wouldn't drink or smoke weed around them, although I did smoke cigarettes. Some of these elders like Vanessa's mother and father went only to the 6th grade. They made up for their shortcomings through hard work, dignity, and self-respect.

Mr. and Mrs. Harris, Mrs. Viola, a single mother raising her grandchildren for a daughter who got strung out on drugs, and later murdered, Mrs. Oneida Lovings, a single mother of ten, Mrs. Jerri, a mother of five, and along with many others became dear friends of mine. Vanessa had four sisters and four brothers. Her older sister Adie Bell, a high school grad, was married to Raymond Smith aka Night Train. They also lived in the East Terrace. Night Train became one of my mentors. He was an Air Force Vet who served in Vietnam. He shared a lot of wisdom with me despite his battle with alcoholism.

Vanessa's brothers Lonnie and Felton Jr. also took me under their wings. Vanessa was dating Drummond Jr., who along with her two brothers were starting to use heroine. I had not encountered this drug back home, but I had heard about its devastation from music artists like James Brown, and Gil Scott Heron. black music and black films educated me about the danger of certain drugs. I wanted no parts of it. I would learn later that the ring of users in the East Terrace was beyond the three mentioned, and it was growing. Most of us stuck to weed and alcohol. Some of the girls would play crazy to get a doctor to prescribe them valiums and quaaludes. I tried both, but I didn't like the lethargic feeling I got. I was too energetic for them.

Little did I know back then how vulnerable our people would be when President Ronald Reagan and his cronies released crack cocaine into our community in 1984. It was the Lebanese magazine, Ash-Siraa that uncovered the Iran-Contra operation on November 3, 1986. Later, drug king pin, Rick Ross testified about his part in the drug trade that funded the Iran-Contra scheme. Col. Oliver North stopped short of revealing his part in the drug operation in a hearing before Congress on July 9, 1987, according to the AmericanRhetoric.com. This government action by President Reagan devastated black communities throughout this country. I saw the ripple effect as I traveled to Dallas, Little Rock, Savanah, Georgia, Memphis, Atlanta, Chicago and other towns. Crack cocaine struck black professionals as well. D.C. Mayor Marion Barry, and former Congressman Julian Bond attest to that. It wreaked havoc on the lower income people. I'll say more about that later. This incident should warn black people and Americans in general, about the dangers of a ruthless president and their co-conspirators.

Back at the Job Corp I was finishing up my training. I was to complete everything by September of 1975. My World of Works class taught me how to budget and manage my money once I got a job. When a corpsman finishes a trade, he/she is sent to the placement center to be placed on a job. One day I was told that I had an interview with masters of the Food City Super Market in San Antonio. I was overcome with anxiety and expectation. I was driven to the Food City Corporate office in 1975, where I met Mr. Joe Hernandez. He looked over my meat cutting certificate and training skills. I thought my lack of a GED would disqualify me, but when he returned, he said "You got the job." I shook his hand and assured him that I would do a good job. My word was my bond, and it is to this day.

I began working on the north side of town on Eisenhower Road. This was a predominantly white area. I landed an apartment in a trailer park and ran into an old girlfriend I had met at Poppy Lounge. Martha was a shapely, dish water blond, white girl who had spent time out in California. She was about twenty-five at the time. I spent time with her at her trailer. We would smoke weed and express our goals and make out. The sexual revolution was in full swing. I managed to buy me a $300 dollar Dodge Coronet that had only one radio channel, 55 KTSA, the same white station we listened to in Job Corps. It played all the latest White jams like Philadelphia Freedom by Elton John, The Best of my Love by the Eagles and Silly Love Songs by Paul McCartney. I fell in love with these songs and my new life.

This good life lasted for about three months. Old Sarge at the Northside Food City Super Market came to me one day and said "Son you have been doing a great job here, and you are always on time. But business has been slow. The store is barely breaking even. I'm going to have to lay you off until things improve. I'll be happy to put in good words for you, should you find another job. Sorry son." And with that, he gave me my pink slip. My rent was paid up for the month, but I had to think fast. I had met a charming young lady on the West side of town named Annette. She was a little on the plump side but had a beautiful face and personality. She lived with her mother, stepfather, and little brother named Mann.

I went over and explained my situation to her and told her I needed a temporary place to stay until I found another job. I knew Smoky and Henry, a couple of older guys in the neighborhood, who might help me find work. Annette's mother agreed to take me in. After about two weeks I got a call from old Sarge telling me I could come back to work. Luckily for me, Annette's stepfather worked near the store, so I caught a ride with him every day. Everything was fine until Annette started telling me she was pregnant, and it seemed like her mother was trying to force us into matrimony. That wasn't in the cards for me, I thought. So, I made plans to pack my things and get out of there. By now I had been laid off again, and things were not looking good. For a minute I was contemplating returning to West Helena. But I couldn't run away from life with my tail tucked between my legs.

For that night I had to put myself up at the Alamo. I waited until after hours and scaled the wall. I found a comfortable bench and went to sleep. I got up just before daylight and started walking around downtown. Man was I hungry and broke. For the first time I realized I was homeless. I called on an old friend I had met while I was in Job Corps named Katie. She spoke with her big sister Cora who welcomed me into her three-room apartment in the East Terrace, right down the street from Vanessa. Cora and her boyfriend Billy received me with open arms. I assured her that when I got my job back, I would pay her to let me stay there. Soon I met Katie's brother Buddigee. He was a player like me, a lady's man, and spoiled rotten by his sisters. But he became one of my best friends.

Cora worked in healthcare. She had a little son we called Pop. She was also taking care of her sister's 14-year-old Katie and 11-year-old Jackie. This became my family. I cracked a lot of jokes, and I guess I had a pretty interesting story. Everyone in the house smoked weed except Pop, who was around 2 years old at the time. I had been sent to work at another Food City store on the southwest side on Zarzamora Street. I would take the transit out there. My boss was called Sarge just like the last Shop supervisor. He was a nice guy, and so was the head butcher, a Mexican American lady's man Mr. Gonzalez. Mostly Mexican Americans worked there serving mostly Mexican American customers. Except for their language they seemed to mimic white people.

I noticed throughout San Antonio, Texas, Mexican Americans were running things. Mayor Lila Cockrell was the mayor, but she was soon to be defeated by Henry Cisneros. And Henry B. Gonzalez was a powerful Congressman representing the area. I liked both Mexican leaders, because I heard them quote Dr. Martin L. King Jr. Mayor Cockrell seemed like a wonderful person also. I was not very political at the time and not that interested. These were the great heydays of black Congresswoman Barbara Jordan. J.D. Sutton was also a great black leader, so much so that they named a housing project after him. I lived with Vanessa at 105 Lena Horne Walk in the Sutton Homes before I joined the Army. Rev. Rector, pastor of Antioch Baptist church on the Eastside along with Pastor Griffin of St. Stephens Baptist church where I attended church, were two strong community leaders at this time. But this was a drop in the bucket compared to the representation of Mexican Americans. Many of the names of streets, buildings, businesses, and historic sites bear the names of Mexican Americans or white Americans. This is not a complaint. It's an observation. I didn't realize at the time how critical it was for black people to assert themselves politically and economically or run the risk of being completely trampled over by those who were more active in these areas. Still, there were black folks there who held their own.

I watched those Baptist preachers and other preachers walk the tight rope between community activism and caring for the spiritual needs of the church goers. It is a daunting task, yet a necessary one. I was too blind to realize at the time that I was contributing to the moral collapse of the community I had come to love so much. Jesus said so eloquently in Matthew All who do not gather with me, scatters abroad. I was certainly not gathering with Christ. And it would be a while before my eyes would become opened to my destructive behavior.

I would be dog tired getting off the transit bus from work each night, but things at Cora's house were changing. There were times when I wouldn't see Buddigee for days. Cora would always come home with the same old smile even though Billy was becoming restless. One night we were smoking weed and I got to learn a little bit about him. He was always friendly toward me. He said he came from Lubbock, Texas. We would walk up to Church's Chicken to get a two piece with jalapeno peppers after we got the munchies from the weed. One day he asked to borrow ten dollars. I gave it to him and didn't think twice about it.

As time went by, I was introduced to Cora's cousin Marshall (23) and Maurice (27). They had large, well-kept, afros. They dressed nicely too. They needed a place to lie low for a while. I came in one night and saw Maurice nodding and leaning as if he would fall to the floor, but he never did. The next night I saw Marshall in the same condition. Another time I saw Maurice running up the stairs carrying a heavy TV. And on another occasion, he would be carrying a turntable. I soon realized that both of those handsome young brothers were strung out on heroin. They had been breaking into people's houses to steal merchandise to sell to buy more smack. Why didn't they just go out and get a job? What about the quality of life? They had sold out to drugs. But when I talked to them on days that they weren't high or in pursuit of the drug, they were the nicest, most intelligent brothers I had ever met.

One day as I sat in the living room, I heard celebratory voices downstairs in the hallway. Mommy's home! Katie, Jackie, and Cora were standing around this large dark-skinned woman dressed in what seemed to be a man's khaki shirt and jeans. She wore a short, cropped afro with a big smile on her. I soon learned that this was Betty their mother, who had just been released from prison. She had caught a narcotic case. I introduced myself. She was very kind to me, and she was crazy about little Pop. He was her little "Diggems Snap" as she called him. She was glad to be home after about five years in prison. She would send me to the store to pick up items for her on occasions. I'm not sure where she got the money, but she bought a nice tan 1970 Eldorado Cadilac, and I loved driving it to the store.

One day I came in, and I saw her nodding and scratching her face, and arms. She had two visitors Joanne and Lamb. I would soon learn that they were Betty's suppliers, and they too were strung out on heroin just like Maurice and Marshall. They were like vampires in need of blood when the urge came on. Maurice and Marshall were breaking into people's houses and doing anything they could to get a fix. I would hear other tenants in the East Terrace complaining about being burglarized by some dope fiend. I had a clue about who the suspect(s) were, but I wanted no involvement.

I also knew that this was not the environment I wanted to live in. One evening I was standing in front of Cora's house and Billy walked up. I had been asking him about my ten dollars. I asked him again, but this time he shouted, "Didn't I tell you I ain't got no damn money!" He pulled out a .38 pistol and put it to my head. I told him to keep the money and I walked away. I went down to Vanessa's house and told Betty Ann what had happened, and that I needed a temporary place to stay. Vanessa and I began fooling around again, even though she was talking to Danny Longshore, Joseph Guy, Snookum, and she still had feelings for Drummond Jr.

An old Job Corps buddy Mickey Williams would come around and give me a ride to see girls. Vanessa's cousin Joyce Nation had a crush on Mickey. But I believe Mickey had entangled himself in an affair with a gay man, and he wasn't so sure about what he wanted. I felt sorry for him. Women loved him, and he and I both loved music and girls, so it seemed. Mickey was one sharp dresser, too. We both loved the latest fashions, and we both had large afros. We would walk downtown just to get phone numbers from the pretty girls. Mickey could charm a bird out of a tree. He would have the girls laughing in no time and introduce one of them to me. We had a smooth game. It was all about having fun. We would take the girls out to a movie, sometimes to an Earth, Wind, and Fire concert, or to a nice club. There was always a possibility that we would run into that right one, someone to truly settle down with, at least that was my thinking.

Singing and becoming a father

I wasn't ready to settle down right then and neither were most of the young ladies I met. These were wild times, filled with excitement. I was ready to get back into music. I was still fascinated with the Jacksons, the Commodores, the O'Jays, Cool and the Gang, and all the groups that came on Soul Train every Saturday at noon. Music was in me, and I had to let it out! I heard some guys harmonizing in the East Terrace, so I started hanging around them and in due time I would meet others. One day I got a chance to sing several Jackson tunes, and caught the ear of Black Mike, a well-known pimp, and his brother, Navy veteran, Jerreal Wayne. The latter was more stable and surer about what he wanted to accomplish musically.

They had a beautiful sister they called Butter Cup. She sang like Gladys Knight. I was impressed and infatuated; except she had a jealous boyfriend named Rodney. We brought in a talented, headstrong falsetto named Bing, who was short with a Napoleon complex. He kept clashing with Jerreal Wayne who also was a falsetto. We soon found a replacement, one easier to work with. Practices went great, but singing opportunities were scarce. San Antonio had a Black radio station with the call letters KAPE. Melvin Waiters aka Marvelous Mel was spinning the soundtracks of our lives during this time. The Isley Brothers *For the Love*, the O'Jays' *She Used to be my Girl*, the Dramatics *Me and Mrs. Jones*, Ohio Players

Roller Coaster, Switch *There'll Never be*, the Commodores *Sweet Love*, and Earth Wind and Fire *Devotion* were hot at the time.

Vanessa assured me she was taking her birth control pills daily. So, there was nothing to worry about when we had sex. I was not fully tuned into what was happening around me. Several young ladies in the East Terrace were getting pregnant. Some were doing it just to get their independence from their mothers. They wanted their own apartment with their own welfare check. Others were getting pregnant to trap their boyfriends. Sometimes it worked and sometimes it did not work.

I believe Jeanette was counseling some of these girls to get pregnant. Most of the girls she was close to, including Vanessa, became pregnant around the same time. Squeaky Lovings became pregnant by Coffee; her sister Shirley became pregnant by Dale; his brother Michael impregnated Vanessa's sister Mary Lee; Patricia Lovings became pregnant by Thomas. I had been going to St. Phillips College to get my GED, but to no avail. One day, Vanessa met me there and we walked back home. I remember telling her that I really wanted to finish school and get a decent job paying better wages. She was quiet as we walked. Finally, she said *"I have something to tell you."* I asked, *"What's that?"* She said, *"I'm pregnant."* I said *"You can't be. You are on the pill."* She said, *"I missed my period."* My heart sank. I said *"Well you will need to get an abortion. I can't have no kid right now."* She didn't say anything. I was wondering even if it was my child. That brought my whole world to a complete standstill. How could this have happened to me? I was not in love. I was only 17. How was I going to take care of a child? I vowed not to follow in my father's footsteps and have a child out of wedlock. This couldn't be happening to me. I was devastated and didn't know the way forward. I accused Vanessa of trapping me with a baby. By now, Mickey and I had gone in together to rent an efficient apartment on WW White Road. I had a job at Stull chemical company making $2.10 an hour. I had a decent used car to get to work and chase girls.

One night Mickey and I brought two girls over for the night; one called herself Ice Cream, and the other Strawberry. The next morning Ice Cream was complaining about Mickey not being able to perform. Strawberry and I thought it was hilarious. Mickey was all talk, and no show. Suddenly, there was a loud knock on the door. I looked out the window and it was fully pregnant, Vanessa breathing threats to kill Strawberry. I went outside to calm her down, while Mickey got the girls into the car because Vanessa was very jealous with a mean temper.

What kind of mess did I get myself into? I felt sorry that she was pregnant, knowing I played a part in it, but I was not ready to give up my freedom, and become a one-woman man. Vanessa seemed to have felt that carrying my child entitled her to me. I had not decided what to do about the newly altered relationship. Should I do like Coffee and my pimp friend Black Mike and leave, visiting my child from time to time? Or could I grow to love Vanessa, and make her my choice with whom to settle down? When I came around her family, I felt pressured by them to take Vanessa for a wife. I began wondering if this was all orchestrated. This feeling haunted me over the years

I had been taking the bus out to Bexar County hospital with Vanessa for her periodic checkups, when one day her water broke, and she had to be rushed to the hospital. My daughter could wait no longer. It was February 20, 1977, when we heard her scream. Once she was cleaned up and Vanessa was resting calmly, I got my first glimpse of her. She looked like the Mexican American babies. I saw my slanted eyes and knew without a doubt she was mine. I held Vanessa's hand as she lay in the bed, still unable to fully process what was happening. Life was moving me like a strong current and all I could do was flow with it.

Vanessa didn't seem to share my frustration. Perhaps because she knew this was her plan. I had no intentions of being faithful. We would argue about the smallest thing. By now she had moved into an apartment in the East Terrace across the yard from her parents on Del Rio Walk. I would stay there sometimes, but other times I lived at my apartment on WW White Road. We had such a heated argument one day, Vanessa told me *"If we break up, Immo make sure you never see your child again!"* She seemed so vindictive that she probably would carry out the threat. I had become attached to my child and Vanessa knew it. At night I would lie in my bed thinking about her future, looking forward to the day that she met my mother and siblings.

I spent more time at Vanessa's, even babysitting sometime when she had to handle some business. I didn't like her being on welfare, but she had a roof over my daughter's head and food to sustain her. Vanesa dropped out of school in the 11th grade to have our child. She had dreams of being a nurse after working at Walter Reed Hospital at Ft. Sam Houston. She liked working and having her own money. As we lived together, I began to see more of her qualities. There were days we would take the baby for a walk. Pushing the stroller gave the appearance of a happy solid family. Friends would wave and stop to see the baby. But Vanessa and I knew the truth. At times we would get along and even go out for the evening.

I was getting more serious about singing now. A group of us guys used to get together and practice at a car wash next door to the Little Hut Night Club, across the street from the New Life Village Apartments. The owner of that club, named Billy, was black with mixed ancestry. He had long wavy salt and peppered hair and spoke with a raspy voice. He decided to have Friday night Gong Shows backed by a band called Life and Death. We called them Life or Death on account they could make you sound good or bad on a Gong Show. Bobby Shark was the entertainer before the Gong Show started. He would do some of Sam Cook's old tunes as well as others. He had a very charismatic style and was definitely a hit with the ladies.

As soon as you walked into the club you could see the stage in the left corner and the bar was on the right. Behind the bar mixing the drinks was a good friend Junior Gibbens. He was a gay man and very kind. He knew everybody in the East Terrace, and everybody knew him. He would give you the shirt off his back. I was proud to call him a friend. The first night I attended the Gong Show, a great singer and friend Ricky Williams got on the stage and sang the O'Jays hot new tune *Money*. He rocked the whole house. But after the crowd settled down, a twenty-two-year-old, thick, church singer got up there and sang Natalie Cole's *Inseparable*. When she hit that high note, everybody stood to their feet and clapped like there was no tomorrow.

The crowd called for an encore. Someone else followed her but it didn't matter. She won the $100 dollar prize that night. And she would make special guest appearances afterwards. Billy was on to something big. The club would be packed out after that. I got up my nerves through the prompting of some friends to sing *Easy* by the Commodores. I had heard Bobby sing it, and I loved the way the band played it. So, one night after downing a rum and coke I went behind the stage and gave Billy my name. Billy went to the stage with his list and announced, "*Let's bring up Sputnik to the stage!"* The butterflies were doing a number in my stomach, but I somehow mustered the courage to walk on the stage. The bright stage lights were blinding. I could not see the audience. Finally, the music started, and I broke out with my first line, and the crowd showed approval. By the time I reached the crescendo *'I wanna be high, so high,"* everyone was on their feet. And I let them have the whole loaf. When I finished, all I heard *was clapping and the chants of "Encore! Encore!" Billy followed behind me saying, "Sputnik, they want an encore."* I turned around and sang it again. I won the badly needed $100 dollars that night. People shook my hand and patted me on the back as I returned to my seat. Certain musicians wanted my phone number and offered to recruit me into their bands. That was a glorious night, a feeling I never had before. I was determined to keep it going. I did guest appearances after that while many of my friends from the East Terrace were in attendance including Vanessa. I was, and am, grateful for that opportunity to sing at Little Hut Night Club.

Becoming a father was a new challenge. I had been singing with different bands around San Antonio, New Braunfels, Seguin, and other towns on the weekend, and working minimum wage jobs during the week, but that was not enough now that I had a baby. I had to consider my daughter in everything I did now. I had asked Vanessa to get an abortion, but I'm so glad she refused. My daughter is so precious to me, and she was the minute I laid eyes on her. Our children are not responsible for what parents do. We owe them pure love when they come into this cruel world. I had to make some decisions. By now, I was working for Mr. Delores Montez's Sprinkler Company. I began working for him after I was fired from the San Antonio City Golf Course. My transportation couldn't get me to the last job on time.

With Montez Sprinkler, I had a friend and a salary. Delores Montez had been my boss at the San Antonio City golf course. He tried to save me from being fired but to no avail. I was still renting my apartment on WW White Road. After **Aundria** (so named for my cousin who saved my life) was born, my sister Rita came down and moved in with me at my invitation. My plan was to help her find a job, and together we would bring my mother to San Antonio in search of a better life. Rita had given birth to my niece Patonya. When she arrived she had brought a friend with her, Mary Alice, who had three children of her own. My apartment was too small for all of them so my sister had to return to West Helena.

The movie *Roots* (1977) had the nation buzzing around the time my daughter was born. It is said that during the week of its viewing, crime dropped in most of the major cities. I couldn't wait to watch each episode. This movie had a lasting impact on me psychologically. It heightened my awareness of ongoing racism. It also gave me a greater appreciation for family. When I was little, I heard a constant question from the elders, "*Who are your people?*"

This question was posed mostly to young boys and girls, but it was also asked of strangers to learn of their connection to our town. I've not studied extensively on slavery, but after reading certain biographies and testimonies by former slaves I believe this question was used heavily by them to reconnect with family members who had been sold off to other plantations. I observed my Aunt Vannie's interaction with other African Americans in our town over the years, and I have seen her make inquiries about people's kinship as well as explaining the kinship of others; for example, around 2013 I was home visiting, when she and I walked into Kelley's restaurant to have breakfast. We ran into one of her old friends, and she started introducing me. She told the woman I was her nephew, and then she said, "*You remember Florine's daughter Glen, don't you?*" Her friend said, *Oh yeah, Glen! I remember her now.* "*Well, this is Glen's boy Sputnik!*" Even as a grown man I still get a tingling sensation when my lineage is verified by an elder. There is this deep sense of connection that comes with it, a kind of validation of one's humanity within the group.

I gained discipline, developed new skills, and broadened by knowledge in the Army

It was when I went into the Army on November 13, 1979, that I found the discipline needed to go back to school. I had been working minimum wage jobs around San Antonio, and singing in night clubs, hanging out with people like me who wanted more out of life. Here's some background, It was February 20, 1977 and it was hitting me that my girlfriend, Vanessa Franks and me were with child. Aundria demanded that I step up my game and provide her with a decent environment. I named my daughter after Marilyn's daughter, the one I credit with saving my life that Friday when the West Helena 4 met their fate. Vanessa and I were a couple, but man did we have some problems. At 17 I was not ready to settle down, nor did I want a child. But unbeknownst to me, she had decided that she was going to get pregnant and forge a union. The pain was suffocating at times,

But I was thoroughly convinced that it was partly my fault too. This hardship forced me to make necessary changes. I was determined not to leave my child the way my father left us. Family is very important to me, so I had to work harder to establish a secure future for us. Vanessa and I had been washing dishes at Ft. Sam Houston Army Base, I was impressed with the nice cars the soldiers were driving. I had managed to buy a used Ford Elite on credit but making $1.80 an hour 26 hours a week was not enough to keep up the payments on the car and an apartment, so I turned to selling marijuana to supplement my income. Even this was not enough. Plus, I ran the risk of getting arrested. I woke up one September morning and found my car was gone. I lived off and on with Vanessa in the Sutton Holmes Project, so I figured someone had stolen it. I called the police to file a report. I called Ford Motor Credit who informed me that the car had been repossessed because of nonpayment. Man was I angry.

I decided now would be a good time to inquire about joining the Army. I took the VIA transit downtown and filled out the paperwork. Luckily the Army was accepting applicants without a GED. I scored high enough to enroll into the Military Police program. I had no clue about what I was embarking upon.

I boarded a plane with another recruit, Jim Becker, and headed for Atlanta. Jim was a polite, quiet, white San Antonian just as anxious as I was. Neither of us knew what to expect. We were to touch down in Atlanta and board a bus for Ft. McClelland, Alabama. We arrived at night. The bus was completely full as we drove down I-20 toward Anniston, Alabama. We entered the gates. Someone at the front of the bus said jokingly "If you want to change your mind, now is the time!" I was wondering if I had made a grave mistake. I think we all had doubts.

The bus came to a stop in a parking lot. The driver pulled up the hand brakes and opened the door. A drill sergeant stepped onto the bus and said "Good evening, ladies and gentlemen Welcome to Ft. McClelland, Alabama. I'm your drill instructor, and you got one minute to get off this bus and thirty seconds is already gone. Get off this damn bus!" And with that, everyone started grabbing their bags and hustling to the front exit. We were rushed to a section of the parking lot in a kind of formation. Some of us had placed their bags on the ground. The drill sergeants came up to them screaming in their ears, "Who told you to put your bags on my ground. Get em up!" We were all standing there holding our bags. The Sergeant said, "Listen up!" as he began barking out orders. I remember thinking to myself, "What have you gotten yourself into this time."

I had a big luster-curl afro, ready to impress any pretty girl that came along. But no one was in the mood for flirting now. We were transported to an orientation center and put up in barracks. Early the next morning we were processed in, filling out paperwork, and watching films. Later we were taken to the barber shop. The barber asked me how I would like my hair to be cut. I told him to keep it even and round. He took those clippers and shaved me bald, and then said "Next!" as he broke into laughter. The Army had a one size fit all haircut for men. Uniformity was the name of the game from then on. We went to get fitted for our uniforms. We received a duffle bag filled with our new clothes and footwear.

The next morning, we all looked like fresh recruits wearing brand new Army greens and black shiny boots. We were taught how to walk, dress, line up for formation, stand at attention, and be at parade rest. After a week of this we began basic training at a new set of dormitories. I was in Bravo Company, or Company B. I was standing in line one morning to get breakfast, and a female drill sergeant came up to me looking very closely at my neck and chin. She said, "Looks like someone forgot to shave this morning. Get out of my line and go and shave! And see me before you get in line to eat." I ran back upstairs to shave. Why was she picking on me? I wondered. That feeling I had reminded me of the white teacher back at Eliza Miller demanding I turn around for a paddling. This was not the place to catch an attitude. I came back down and passed her inspection, but not without hearing a mini lecture from her. I said very little. But she didn't like it. "Get out of my line!" she said. I could see that she was going to be a problem. I also knew how much my mouth had gotten me in trouble before, like the time I was kicked out of school. I decided to start holding my peace and get through Basic Training. My strategy worked. In the Army, they call it keeping a low profile.

Weeks of training went by quickly. We began at 5 a.m. each morning with shaving, brushing our teeth, making up our beds, and getting dressed. By 5:30 a.m. we were all downstairs in-formation, ready to do PT. Sometimes I was a road guard. Staff Sergeant Williams Owens was our drill instructor. He would call cadence for a brief period, and then he would call on one of us to do it. After learning all the songs, I felt confident that I could do it. One morning when he asked who will call cadence for us? I said, "I will Drill Sergeant!" He said, "Well, come on out here then Wheeler!" I started off in the familiar rhythmic call and response cadence, and all the troops responded back approvingly.

Soon, when the morning runs began Sergeant Owens would simply say, "Where Wheeler at?" I loved calling cadence, and I loved running. But I remembered to keep a low profile otherwise. We went to chow after the morning run and then training. Training shut down for Christmas. Many of the soldiers and drill instructors went home until after New Years, so those of us who remained were moved to temporary barracks. Our schedule was relaxed, but we could not leave the base. I became sick with strep throat and hemorrhoids at the same time.

I went on sick call and was given medicine for my ailments. Two MPs showed up one day and asked "Are you Joseph Wheeler? " I said "Yes." He said, "Come with us." And with that I was handcuffed and placed in the back seat of a patrol car. It turned out someone had broken into the Coke machine, and according to a witness, it was me. I tried to explain that I had been sick and had not been near the Coke machine. Finally, they found the real culprit. It was a young Puerto Rican recruit, who looked so much like me that I had to take a double look. The MPs apologized to me and took me back to the barracks. I spent the rest of the holidays writing letters and listening to Michael

Jackson's Off the Wall album. I even wrote to Brenda.

Basic training came to an end, and we soon began our Advanced Individual Training (AIT). We were training to be Military Police Men and Women. We were now allowed to go away on a weekend pass into town. Six weeks of training alongside females, but not being allowed to get too close was a big challenge. As soon as we got into town most of us went to the hotels to party and have fun. We went to Oxford, Alabama about 4 miles down the street. Someone knew where the hottest dance joints were. I was hanging out with a nice young Californian named Vernice Carter. We partied all weekend. When those soldier girls dressed up, they looked totally different from when they wore their battle dress uniforms (BDUs) and some of them looked like they could be on the cover of a fashion magazine. Or then again, maybe we were so glad to be close to girls it just seemed that way. Vernice and I remained friends throughout our Army training, but I was still in love with a San Antonian named Brenda Hughes. She sent me a dear john letter three weeks into my training. Plus, I still had unfinished business with Vanessa and my newborn. That part of my life was a bit twisted.

One of the cadences I heard caused me to reflect hard about going to war. The cadence took its pattern from the hook Poison Ivy by the Coasters. It went like this: Iran, Iran, late at night while you're sleeping bravo company come a creeping Iran, Iran. I came into the Army a few months after the Iranians had taken 52 American hostages and were holding them ransom. The threat of war was imminent according to most of the drill instructors, so emphasis was placed on staying alive and learning combat skills for survival. We had one night training exercise where we drove our jeeps in blackout conditions up a steep hill. When we reached the summit, we assembled at bleachers in the dark. A certain training NCO came before us and scared the living hell out of us with stories about his service in Vietnam.

This Vietnam vet/instructor talked about seeing his buddies get blown away by various explosive devices and having to stuff his friend's intestines back into his body as his friend shivered in his arms. He walked closer to us and looked at a certain soldier and said, "I don't think you will make it back alive," and then he looked at the rest of us and said, "You gone die, all of you!" It was a serious wake up call. Fun time was over. Before this time, I saw the Army as a chance to learn a new trade or a career and return home to make an above minimum wage salary. Now I started paying attention to the news. I was watching the presidential campaign between Ronald Reagan and Jimmy Carter. Some on the right was trying to cast Carter as weak on Iran, while praising Reagan for being strong and taking a tough stance. It occurred to me that one of these two guys would have a direct effect on my life for the next three years. I think I voted for the first time in that upcoming election.

I was not political at the time, but I had so many

questions swarming around in my head, such as why the Iranians at Lackland Air Force Base in San Antonio trained to fly F-16 fighter jets and learning other combat skills. I used to see Iranian men downtown at the pub drinking and dancing together. They would be dressed in civilian clothes at the pub. But I had a chance to talk to some of them and learned a little bit about their culture. I remember seeing images of Iranians in their homeland protesting, burning U.S. flags and chanting "Death to America!" They called our country the great Satan, and other derogatory names. What happened? How did the relationship turn sour? Google and smart phones didn't exist back then. I didn't bother to research the subject. It would be many years later that I learned about the CIA's involvement in the coup of 1953. They fomented tension between certain factions in the country that led to the overthrow of a popular democratically elected leader named Mosaddegh. This Iranian leader took back the oil fields from the British and nationalized them. This did not sit well with the British, so they enlisted the aid of the U.S. to help shore up Western Control. The U.S. involvement in Iranian political affairs boiled over during the 1979 Iranian revolution which led to the capture of 52 American hostages. The Russians also wanted in on the control of the oil fields, so one could argue that the cold war played a role. I came to view it as colonialism gone awry. The Army encourages soldiers to do research on a subject.

But following that night-exercise, I knew I had to work on building up my psychological defenses. Up until then, my life was about getting high, partying down every weekend, and chasing girls. Now I was being called on to be patriotic. What did that mean? Yes. I raised my right hand and swore on the Bible to defend the US Constitution against all enemies foreign and domestic. But what did that mean? I had never fully read the US Constitution let alone scrutinize all the inconsistencies surrounding it. But now I was about to give my life for it. I believe that a person learns more in the Army in six weeks than some college students learn in a year. I certainly did. We saw films about the Geneva Convention and how to conduct oneself in the theatre of war. We discussed atrocities committed by combatants as far back as the civil war.

We looked at footage taken in the Vietnam war of soldiers killing innocent civilians, or prisoners of war. We saw extreme interrogation tactics that were unlawful. And because I was going to be a military policeman, I would be called on to enforce the Uniform Code of Military Justice (UCMJ) as well as international laws provided by the likes of the Geneva Convention. Military training forces one to grapple with the reality of the battlefield. I was gradually becoming a soldier. But I was also gradually becoming political.

In the Army we were constantly reminded to pay attention to detail. We were told that if a superior officer asked us a question about a matter and we didn't know the answer, we were to respond by saying "I don't know the answer, but I will find out." I began the practice of researching subjects of which I had no knowledge. I had no access to marijuana or alcohol during these six weeks of basic training and it must have allowed my mind to be freed up. The hands-on training in the Army accelerated my thinking also. The drill instructors demonstrated everything and then brought each of us up to try it. Some of the soldiers were clearly advanced in their education, and they excelled rapidly. I needed all the help I could get.

After basic training we received our certificates of completion, and we began our Advanced Individual Training. The Military Police Academy was very structured. It involved reading, critical analyses, and physical engagement. We had to know when to use deadly force, how to conduct a traffic accident investigation, rescue people, protect a crime scene, investigate a crime scene, charge a person under the Uniform Code of Military Justice, local laws, state laws, federal laws, international laws, etc. We had to complete several modules successfully before we could graduate. By the end of AIT, I was not the same person anymore. I broke with Sputnik. I was Private, soon to be Private First-Class Joseph Wheeler. Some of us went into town on the last weekend of training and our final stay at Ft. McClelland, Alabama. We celebrated. I learned that at least four of my fellow cadets would be stationed at Ft. McPherson in Atlanta Georgia with me. Others were going to South Korea,

Germany, Panama, and other parts of the country and world.

I observed that some of our drill instructors were now in a more relaxed state. I thought these drill Instructors were an awesome, disciplined bunch. Each was committed to their work. Never in my life had I encountered such dedication. I had to tip my hat. I was looking forward to applying my newly acquired skills as a military policeman. For once in my life, I felt important. I wore my uniform with great pride and confidence. I would return to San Antonio for two weeks bearing this great sense of accomplishment. I had so much to share with Vanessa, her family, and my friends. They were all going to be amazed, or so I thought.

But when I did return to San Antonio in 1980, there was no celebration. Everyone was still doing the same thing ... surviving. A priority for me was to get Vanessa and my daughter out of the Sutton Homes Projects. An old friend of the family, Edward Perkins, had robbed Vanessa at gun point while I was in basic training. She was standing there holding my crying two-year-old while he robbed her. He too, had gotten strung out on heroin; otherwise, he was the nicest person you ever wanted to meet. In fact, he ended up marrying Vanessa's sister Louise. I had learned of the tragic news about a good friend black Albert who was shot in the head 1978 by people we knew, and another good friend Peter Stein had been killed that same year before we moved out of the East Terrace project.

Violence was starting to increase in the black community there. And it was alarming. I feared for my family's safety.

I went to visit old friends at their homes and at the night clubs. They all wondered where I had been. We talked, but I realized that our conversations were so far apart now. Much of what I was saying was boring to them. I knew the routine, for that was my lot before my big break. Years later, after I read the philosopher Plato's The Analogy of the Cave, which was powerful, and caused me to reflect on this period of my life. I'm paraphrasing, but Plato said that being enlightened can be likened to people in a cave chained to the wall, and behind them is an opening which allows light into the cave. Shadows appear on the wall in front of them to which they give names. Ultimately, they developed a tradition around these figures. But one of them broke away and went through the opening. It hurt his eyes at first, but soon he realized that there were people and animals passing by the opening casting shadows on the wall in the cave. He returned to the cave to inform his friends about what he saw and to give them an explanation for the shadows they were seeing. But his friends became angry with him and accused him of going away and learning some outlandish doctrine. They defended their myths and traditions, and refused to allow the light of understanding to come in. This is how I felt during my visits with my old friends. I even tried to encourage several to join the military if for no other reason than to get the benefits or get out of San Antonio.

The military forced me to reflect on certain issues, such as Black Nationalism, the civil rights movement, desegregation, political systems, economic systems, etc. These ideas had always been in my thinking, but I didn't read enough to investigate them. Yet in the Army these subjects were discussed and thrusted in my face, causing me to learn more. I did encounter racists in basic training, but they were trainees like me, and therefore posed no threat. Under President Carter we had to assemble in a circle to talk about race. The Army's policy was that everyone wearing the uniform was green, and racism would not be tolerated. Even though there were pockets of racist acts, I felt that most of my peers and superiors alike were fair minded people. I was never treated unequally in all my interactions with people. It seemed that there was one Army.

In Basic training one day during PT, Drill Sgt. Stacey Statham said, "Look at ya, a bunch of commies!" He went on about the old Army not allowing trainees to get away with stuff we were getting away with. I kept looking for ways the communists were influencing our military. Had the communists infiltrated the upper echelon? I knew I was not a communist. Hell, I didn't even know the meaning of the word. I just knew Russia and China were communists, and other Eastern bloc countries because we had to study their tanks and fighter jets' insignias, so I knew the communists were the enemy.

I had not read Karl Marx, Mao, or Lenin. I didn't know much about Cuba except that the U.S. despised Fidel Castro, and I wondered why. There was only one other person or group that I had heard white folks call communists, and that was Martin L. King Jr., other civil rights leaders, and groups like the NAACP, the Black Panthers, etc. I certainly identified with the latter two groups, though I was not actively involved with either. I was only 9 years old when Dr. King was assassinated. Was Drill Sergeant Statham expressing his white pride? Was he railing against President Carter's zero tolerance for racism? It was not clear to me. But the racial climate in the Army was tolerable during the Carter years, at least for me.

I arrived at Ft. McPherson in Atlanta, Georgia on April 1, 1980, the beginning of my 21st birthday. I was assigned my dorm room housed in an old WW I barracks, across from the Orderly Room. First Sergeant King greeted me. He was a light-skin brother from Memphis, Tennessee, my neck of the woods. He was laid back walking around with a cup of coffee in his hand. The hash marks on his uniform told me he had already served 18 years or more. He was highly polished. Rarely did I see my company commander. His secretary, a young black female kept all of us straight and out of trouble. Our Operation Sergeant was Staff Sergeant Hester, a big white guy who spoke with a Southern drawl. He was firm, quick witted, and good natured. His humor could disarm you, but he was all Army. The trees were starting to bloom around Hedekin Field. Across the field was General's Row, a row of handsome WW II houses fit for the generals. Hedekin Field was kept manicured. This was where we had numerous high-profile retirements, change of command, or promotion ceremonies.

Ft. McPherson was all garrison duty, which meant there was no combat training except for what we received from books and films. We handled retirement and change of command ceremonies. We worked three days on, three days of classroom training, and three days off. When working, our shifts were day shift (7 a.m. to 3 p.m.), swing shift (3 p.m. to 11 p.m. or midnight shift (11 p.m. to 7 a.m.). We wore our khaki tans or mint green short sleeves and Class A pants in summer, and Battle Dress Uniforms (BDUs) on the midnight shift. There were many days we would finish class early and go on what the sergeants called "escape and evasion," which meant leaving the area, and be out of sight out of mind. Some of us would go downtown to the Omni and watch people figure skate while we eat pizzas and drink beer.

Atlanta had some of the most beautiful young ladies. Nightlife in Atlanta was something to write home about. A few of us guys would ride down Campbellton Road to Markos, Cisco's, or Mr. V's Figure 8 nightclubs. We were dancing to Chic's Good times, Luther Vandross' in the Glow of Love, the Commodores' Brick House, Brick's Jazz Dazz, and many other hot tunes. Like the mid-seventies, the early eighties were a festive time in America. The music tells a lot about how many people were feeling.

We never heard about a shooting at a club. These were places to meet girls, dance, and put the work week in the rearview mirror. Everyone was dressed in the latest fashions. The disco music was still king. I was not so worried about the threat of war. Although I would tune in to the news now and then. I had a couple of lady friends I went out with on weekends, but nothing serious.

I went into the orderly room soon after I arrived at Ft. McPherson and saw a familiar face in a picture on the bulletin board. It was an old childhood friend named Melton Parker. Back home we called him Beaver. I enquired about him and learned that his squad was on the night shift. I got up early the next morning and greeted him. It was a happy reunion. I learned that he and his wife Cynthia were living in an apartment at Holland Park located at Ft. Gillem. We patrolled both installations. He helped me get Vanessa and my daughter processed in. They had been living at Ft. Sam Houston in San Antonio, Texas. According to Army regulations, a couple had to be married to get additional money for families, so on May 9, 1980, Vanessa and I went downtown Atlanta and got married at the courthouse. It increased my paycheck by around $200 a month, and it allowed me access to an apartment that I could afford at Ft. Gillem. Mel, Cynthia, their son Little Mel, and my family did many things together. We went shopping, had cookouts, and we even exercised together.

The Holland Park community was very family friendly, and very secure, a far cry from Sutton Homes. Finally, Vanessa and I had gotten out of the housing project. We were almost in the middle class it seemed. We had healthcare, good neighbors, and a livable wage job. I managed to buy a used car from a soldier who was leaving for another post. Now I was able to drive back and forth from Ft. Gillem to Ft. McPherson (which was called Ft. Mac by everyone). My MP duties were a piece of cake. Crime consisted of petty larceny at the PX, false alarms at the bank, Class VI (liquor) store, or the NCO club. Most of us MPs were looking for an opportunity to use our training, but very little went on at either of those installations. At Ft. Gillem there were felony larceny cases which we had to turn over to local authorities, because the perpetrators were civilians. We ran radar on Hood Avenue at Ft. Gillem to catch speeders. Usually, I would give the speeder a warning unless he/she was disrespectful. I liken the two posts to Mayberry R.F.D. But even Atlanta was not as crime stricken as it became during the late 80s into the 2000s.

Germany

I loved Ft. McPherson. I wished I could have stayed there throughout my term of service. But that was not to be. I came down on orders to go to Germany after about eleven months. Not only would I have to leave paradise, but I also had to get on an airplane again. I was terrified of airplanes. This would be an eighteen-hour flight. Was there a way I could get out of it? I had a few months to prepare. I had heard that the Army Band members did not get reassigned that often. They practiced across the street from our unit. I would often hear them practicing, and sometimes they would play familiar pop tunes. On some evenings I would go over and listen. One day I got up the nerves to inquire about a possible position in the band. Even though I didn't play an instrument, I sang Lionel Richie's songs well, and I was good with Jeffrey Osborne's tunes and many others.

The band leader was amused. He asked me if I would be willing to change my Military Occupation Specialty (MOS). I asked him to let me think about that one and get back to him. Was I ready to give up my MP career after all that training? Nah. I was not ready to throw in the towel just yet. I needed a job when I left the Army. MP was an occupation I could use back in civilian life. I started going to the post library to check out books on the German language. I watched videos and listened to audios to help with the language. I resolved that I would only have about 13 months left on my Army contract, and then I could either re-enlist or get out. I was leaning heavily toward getting out at the end of my tour. President Jimmy Carter lost the election, and from what I could gather Mr. Reagan was a hard liner. He was talking about cutting government spending and increasing spending for the military. Mr. Carter pointed to his policies that kept America out of war. He talked about his peace initiatives in the Middle East. I felt that the country was in a good place under Mr. Carter, but I was alarmed by Mr. Reagan's rhetoric. My orders said I was being assigned to the 2nd and 1st Air Defense Artillery (ADA) Battery in Wackenheim (pronounced Vacken-hime), Germany. Vanessa and Aundria would have to return to San Antonio and stay in an apartment at Ft. Sam Houston Army base for thirteen months. Even though Vanessa and I were married, we both were mindful of the rugged road that led us there.

I arrived in Germany in the month of October in 1981. I would stay there 13 months. I did a week or two in Frankfurt for processing. I could smell manure, which lingered in the air. After processing in, I was shipped off to Wackenheim. A van dropped us off at the Hauptbahnhof (train station). I had an hour layover. I joined other soldiers at the pub where I was first introduced to altbier (dark beer). I drank a mug and man was it smooth going down, so I decided to have another one. I don't remember anything between that second beer and the time I was dropped off at the entrance to the casern or military base. I knew that the cab was a white Mercedes, and it was raining cats and dogs. In fact, it seems it rain every day straight for about a month. I was told we were in the monsoon season. Someone helped me to the barracks.

The casern or military base had one street about a block long. It had a gate shack at the entrance, a small library, a small chapel, NCO club, and three sets of barracks, about one fifth the size of Ft. Mac. We had more in-processing to do at Wiesbaden (pronounced Vees bodden). We sat in classes to learn to speak Dutch, which is used in Germany, even though German is the official language. I learned about the exchange rate, and the laws and customs. We delivered our medical records to the clinic and received our orders and assignments. Once I reported to the orderly room and learned of my work schedule, I got to know some of the brothers in my dorm. They showed me the ropes. A couple of guys even offered me hashish. I wasn't ready for that yet. I learned that our duties entailed guarding nuclear missiles. We would not be arresting anyone or doing any police work. We didn't even have to worry about surprise urinalysis testing. I had planned to revisit the hashish proposition later. But for now, I was curious about German beer. The NCO club had the best premium pizzas.

There were three fine Gasthaus (pubs/restaurants) in the area. All were in walking distance. I went to one owned by a German named Eric. He had the best

huhnchen (chicken) and pommes frites (French fries).
I can smell that wonderful aroma to this day. In a
Fenten Gasthaus nearby I fell in love with Jager
schnitzel (breaded fried pork chop) with dark brown
gravy and mushrooms topped off with a fresh salad.
The third gasthaus sat in a neighborhood down a hill.
I would join other soldiers there on some Fridays.
They had good pizzas, beer, and a black man who
played the blues on an acoustic guitar. He was a
professional recording artist, who had gotten out of
the military and stayed in Germany. He wore an afro
and a tattered beard. I imagine he was a retiree also.
His companion was a German lady. Some fraulein (a
single German female) seemed curious about African
Americans. I would meet them at discos or downtown
at a pub, or on a train. I had heard guys talking about
the wonderful relationships they had with German
girls. I was invited to the home of a certain fraulein.
We engaged in beautiful conversations about culture,
music, and fashions. They helped me perfect my
Dutch language skills. And I was astonished by the
absence of racial tension. My experience was that
many German people went out of their way to be nice
especially when they saw our respect for their culture
and language.

I was determined to speak only Dutch when I left
the post. I would study it night and day. I had all the
routine phrases and words down pat. I was twenty-
one, interacting with Germans who were eighteen,
nineteen, and sometimes much older. Black music
was playing in all the discos, but I learned to do the

chicken dance at the Oktoberfest as well. I took a boat up and down the Rhine River to view the wine groves, castles, and went on volksmarches or long walks. I visited the first printing press in Gutenberg, and the place where Martin Luther attached his ninety-five theses on a church door in Wittenberg. I tried to learn all I could about Germany. But I avoided discussing the forbidden topics of religion and politics with the German people. Military leaders had sternly warned us about these subjects. I saw a drunk American soldier violate this rule once, and it wasn't pretty.

I was going out with an attractive young African American soldier named Zoan. She lived in barracks across the street. She caught my eye one snowy morning. She was all bundled up in her BDUs ready to go to the field with her unit. I ran out the door to poke fun at her. She laughed and asked me my name. We made plans to go down to the gastehaus for pizza over the weekend when she got back. We MPs did not have to go to the field for Army training, only down range to guard the missiles. My routine began. I was working one day on and one day off. My dorm mates and I would walk down to the 2nd and 1st Air Defense Artillery (ADA) headquarters and assemble for formation. After briefings, we loaded onto a large od green bus, headed out the main entrance, took a right and another right, and went down the side road for about three quarters of a mile to the missile range.

The MP checked everyone in at the gate, and then we had to go through another entrance to the building. It felt like a high security prison except we were all guards and employees and there were no prisoners. We were relieving the off going shift. There were soldiers who maintained the missiles who went to their station, and the MPs had to assume security posts, or prepare for training. Our meals were brought to us from the mess hall. There were four towers in a triangular configuration around the missile compound. Tower one could be accessed without leaving the building, but the other three required a brief walk down a path between two sets of Constantine-wired fences. We took turns of three-hour shifts in each tower. We were to stop any would-be terrorist from getting to the nuclear warheads. Anyone found in the kill zone who did not respond to our commands to halt could be killed on the spot. Of course, there were layers of intelligence and local authority to alert us about suspicious persons in our area. Never did we encounter any terrorists. It was mundane work. Sometimes temper would flare among the lower ranking MPs. We were warned about the effects of alcoholism, although both our platoon sergeant and platoon leader Lt. Stamp battled the disease.

I remember walking back to my dorm one morning, when I saw a white Volkswagen in the parking lot with the engine running. As I got closer, I could see Lt. Stamp inside passed out. I tapped on the window to see if she was alright. She woke up clearly disoriented. She rolled down the window, and I said, "Ma'am, are you alright?" I saw that she was inebriated. She put her car in drive and drove off. This duty affected all of us in some strange way. In addition to the German beer, I would also buy a fifth of Courvoisier at the corner package store. I just didn't care for the hashish. I tried it once, but it was more potent than any weed I'd ever smoked.

We were guarding nuclear missiles, and the cold war was at its height. I was paranoid enough about a possible nuclear war breaking out. I didn't need any help from hashish. I watched two African American MPs have a mental break down while I was there. I was down range when Sgt Ramirez, our squad leader engaged in some kind of horse play with this linebacker of a brother named Meeks. Ramirez was known to get on people's nerves by making them do extra work just because he had the authority. This day Meeks wasn't having it. Ramirez threatened to write him up, and Meeks snapped. A shouting match ensued and the next thing I knew, Meeks had Ramirez pinned against the wall with his M16 A1 assault rifle aimed at Ramirez with a round in the chamber. Tears were streaming down Meeks' face, and no one could reason with him.

The top leaders came into the room. Ramirez was shaking in his boots. Meeks was a friend of mine, but even I was afraid to say something for fear I might set him off. Just a few minutes passed, but it seemed like eternity. Finally, Meeks lowered the weapon. It was taken from his hands, and he sat down on a bunk and cried. He was relieved of his duties and taken to a mental hospital in Frankfurt, Germany. We all joked about Ramirez needing a change of pants after that. He certainly modified his horse playing. For the most part, racism was not a major factor here. I made some wonderful white friends from around the U.S., but occasionally we had disagreements.

I met another brother from Atlanta, who used to lift weights. We went to church together somedays. He was very friendly. We started out having great conversations. I befriended him when he first arrived. Mike spoke of his ambitions after his tour in the Army. I didn't see any signs of mental stress. He fell into the routine of going down range, performing his tower duties. He would get agitated now and then over something someone said to him. And slowly he started complaining about things. One day he said " You're gonna burn in hell!" I thought maybe he was becoming a religious fanatic. But then he began telling everyone, including his superiors. At first, I thought it was some kind of scheme to get out of the Army. I knew he didn't like our assignment there. Nobody did. He ended up having a mental breakdown. I felt sorry for him, but there was nothing I could do to help him. He too was taken to a mental facility in Frankfurt and later processed out.

I was summoned to the orderly room in 1982. I had a message from the Red Cross. I used the company phone to call the Red Cross. I was informed that my brother Jerreal Lee Wheeler had been killed, and that I would be flying back home to attend the funeral. I was numb. I cried as I walked back to my dorm. I questioned God. Why Jerreal, the nice one? I was the sinful one, the one who chased women, smoked weed, hung out in night clubs. Hell, I was the one who introduced Jerreal to smoking and drinking. You took the wrong one, I cried. I was devastated. He and I had planned to meet up in San Antonio and bring our mother, sister and brothers there to start a new life. Now this. I took the long scary flight back to face my sorrow. I learned when I got there that the Red Cross was late getting the message to me. My brother had already been buried. That was another blow.

I left Momma's house in Helena and walked up the street. I saw an old man who looked so familiar. He wore an orange florescent cap; the kind white folks wore when hunting. As I got closer, I could see it was my grandfather, Comer Wheeler. He walked with a cane. I ran fast to catch up to him. I stood in front of him and said "granddaddy!" He looked at me and started crying. He said I had "Ask God to let me see you before I died. Now I can go in peace." I hugged him not knowing that in just a few months my Aunt Melvina would find him dead in his home.

Granddaddy looked like a white man. He was one of the nicest men I knew. His father was white, but he never talked about him. Whites used to threaten his black family for allowing that "white boy to play with those black kids." My father said Granddaddy gave his life pure hell when he was a little boy. But for some reason I was the pride of his old age. I was not sure what that was about, but I loved my grandfather too.

Many days I would go and visit him, and we would walk down to his favorite cafe to have lunch. He would order a fried lunch meat and cheese sandwich for us, and he would drink a Busch beer. He would give me money to play the Jackson 5 songs on the jukebox. All those memories danced in my head as I bid him farewell.

After spending time with my mother, I was off to Germany again to finish off my tour. The death of my brother left me in a mild case of depression. I started going to church to find some consolation. There was a female pastor there we called Evangelist Brown, and man was she on fire for God. When she preached it seemed she was talking directly to me, but I had never met her before. I began reading the Bible and following along with her teachings. I had been trying to learn to play bass guitar. I was even spending time at the recreation center doodling around on the old beat up piano. I taught myself to play Jesus is Love by the Commodores. It was soothing to me. I also created my own original tunes. Evangelist Brown's husband, who was also our cook at the Mess Hall, played the piano at church and sang. I could tell he was struggling with homosexuality, and it seemed like he was winning in Jesus' name. He was a very nice brother who invited me to church services on and off the base.

I met many God-fearing soldiers and their families during this period. I had a lot of baggage. I wasn't getting promoted, I had a learning deficit, I still hadn't gotten my GED, and I only had about five more months to be in the military. I was married to Vanessa, but my heart wasn't completely in it. One night I was sitting on my bunk reading the Bible, and I came across a scripture in the epistle of James 1:5-8. It said if any man lacks wisdom, let him ask of God who gives all things freely and upbraided not. I confronted God and said, if this is true, I am going to get on my knees right now and ask you for wisdom, and if I don't receive wisdom then I am going to conclude that this Bible is nothing but lies. I got down on my knees and asked God to give me wisdom. Soon I started comprehending the Bible in new ways. I read it from cover to cover about five times. I also began taking a correspondence course in criminology by mail, and to my surprise I completed several modules successfully. I turned my transcript in to the personnel office. I was notified by my Platoon sergeant that I was being promoted to E-4. I was a specialist now, making more money. Before I prayed, I could not comprehend what I read. I had a short attention span, but now I was beginning to understand the spirit of the authors behind the words.

I give God the credit for giving me a breakthrough concerning my learning deficit. It had been a problem for me since the fifth grade. I would read history or science but could not process the full meaning of the paragraphs, so when I came to the multiple-choice questions, I would fail each time. But something had changed following that prayer when I asked God for wisdom. One day while I was in the tower overlooking the missiles, I began wondering why Americans were in Germany. And where did the German People come from?

When I got off from work, I went to the library and checked out some books on the subject. I read about Bismarck as well as the causes of WW I and WW II. I began visiting sites such as Gutenberg where the first Bible was printed, and the church in Wurttemberg, where Martin Luther attached his ninety-five theses. I visited Hitler's retreat in Berchtesgaden. I visited Dachau concentration camp and other concentration camps, where Jews had been imprisoned and murdered by the Nazis some thirty-seven years prior. We couldn't drink the local water because of contamination from the bombing during WWII. But that was only one of the scars still prevalent because of the war. I was starting to identify with the human toll as well. Books on the Jewish Holocaust opened my eyes to the devastating war. Reading about Detrich Bonhoeffer challenged me to consider the depth of my Christian beliefs and the commitment it would require when faced with unbridled evil. Bonhoffer, a Protestant theologian, opposed the Nazis who were trying to exterminate the Jews. He stood in the gap and declared the brotherhood and the sisterhood of all humankind. It cost him his life, but he bore his cross just like Jesus to Calvary. I wondered if I could muster such courage. Studying the fall of the Roman Empire fascinated me also. I learned about the barbarians who helped to destroy it. From the tribes of Europe came the nation states of France, Spain, Germany,

Britain, Portugal, Norway, and other places I was becoming familiar with. Many of these were NATO countries established after WWII. Foreign policies were making a little sense to me now.

I bought certain biblical aids to help me learn more about the Bible. Some of my friends were starting to stop by my dorm to hear me espouse on certain truths of the Bible. At times while laying on my bunk, small sermonettes would pop into my head out of nowhere. I envisioned myself speaking to family and friends back home about the virtues of fearing God. I felt a kind of godly sorrow for the destruction I had left behind because of working for Satan. The scriptures were pointing that out.

Proverbs and Ecclesiastes fed my appetite for more wisdom. I knew I was being transformed when an attractive young lady came into my space flirting with me. Her boyfriend Miles had returned to the U.S., and she wanted company. I still had lust in my heart, but the scripture and the knowledge I was gaining neutralized me. I feared that if I indulged in promiscuity, I would lose the favor of God. I found a way to relate that to her, and we agreed to just be friends. The old me was saying "Have you lost your damn mind?" Specialist Aims had a rocking body, beautiful face, and a warm personality. But I was committed to that which had taken hold of me. I continued going to church, praying and fasting sometimes. I read books daily.

Thirty days before my tour ended in 1982, I was

called to personnel and presented with the option of re-enlisting for another three years or ending my tour. I was heavily leaning toward getting out of the military, not knowing whether I would find a decent job or not. I asked the recruiter to give me time to think about it. Once again, I turned to God in prayer. I asked Him point blank if I should get out or stay in. I had three powerful dreams. Each one involved me traveling abroad. In my third dream I was back at my old apartment in San Antonio. I walked out of the door, down the stairs, and between my unit and the building next door, and I found myself in a German city downtown eating with German-speaking ladies. We were all in a festive mood. I understood the meaning of the dreams; I should re-enlist for another three years. This was a hard decision, but I said to God, I'm going to put my trust in you.

Back to Ft. McPherson

So, I re-enlisted and I was sent back to Ft. McPherson, Georgia. Once there, I attended church regularly. I even joined the post gospel choir led by Chaplain assistant, Staff Sergeant Howard E. Franklin. He had also started his own church in an apartment on Stanton Road. Many of us soldiers supported him. It turns out that Franklin too had a major encounter with God while serving in Germany. We shared our testimonies as did other soldiers. I loved singing in the post choir, and the one at church as well. Pastor Franklin eventually moved into a building on Campbellton Road, just outside of Ft. Mac. Those were wonderful church services. Soon Vanessa and my daughter Aundria would join me in Georgia. We moved into another apartment in Holland Park.

I took the time to pursue my GED once again around 1983. I had been taking adult classes at Ft. Mac as we called the base. And to my surprise I was understanding the subjects a lot better now. However, I was still intimidated by the GED test; after all, I had flunked it at least eight or nine times counting the ones in Job Corps. I went to the Atlanta Area Tech College on Stewart Avenue (now Metropolitan Way) to take the test. Weeks went by. I knew for sure I had failed it again. One of the things I wanted most in life was to finish high school. It was a shameful burden that I had been carrying around. I just couldn't score enough points to get it. One day I picked up the mail expecting nothing but bills and advertisements. But there was an awkward looking letter from the Atlanta Area Tech College. I opened it on the spot knowing it was a notice telling me I failed to meet the requirements. I read it carefully, looking for the denial portioned, but a little way down it said congratulations. You have successfully completed the requirements for your GED. A powerful sense of relief came over me. I felt proud. My persistence paid off.

I was in total disbelief at first. I walked into the house and shared the news with Vanessa. Later I shared it with Mel and anyone else who would listen. I was so elated. You'd thought I'd won the lottery. The prayer I prayed back in Germany was still bearing fruit, I thought. My confidence was strong, so I signed up for the Primary Leadership Development Course (PLDC). This three-week training course was held at Ft. Benning near Columbus, Georgia. Extra specialized training meant greater opportunities for promotions.

I completed my training and received a lateral promotion to corporal in 1984. A corporal was a Non-Commissioned Officer (NCO) even though the pay grade was equivalent to a Specialist Four. The Army was beginning to phase out the rank of corporal. Some of the haters called it a glorified Spec 4. I wore my stripes with pride. I was also appointed desk sergeant at Ft. Gillem. Things were really looking up. I was reading more now, and I had more responsibility. One day I made the Sentinel (post newspaper). There I was standing with the Provost Marshal, Lt. Pamela Woods, looking over the MP journal. I kept that article. Our household income increased when Vanessa landed a job at a warehouse at Ft. Gillem. These were the best of times. I wasn't throwing my money away on loose women and night clubs, and I had become a deacon at the Church of Preparation Evangelistic (C.O.P.E.), where Elder Howard E. Franklin was the Overseer.

I was riding down Forest Parkway in Forest Park, Georgia in 1983 when my eyes caught sight of a beautiful white and tan 1978 Grand Prix at a car lot. I pulled in and inquired about it. The next day I went to Bank South at Ft. Mac to try and get a loan. I had always been turned down since my car (add an 'a')? was repossessed back in 1979. But there was beautiful African American woman there named Barbara who said, "I can help you get a loan for that car." She drew up the paperwork, and I drove off the lot with that car. It was the nicest ride I had ever had.

Military life at Ft. Mac was still laid back. Once a gung-ho Staff Sergeant got bored and began flaunting his white privilege by persuading our company commander to let him take the company of MPs on ARTEP in 1983, which stood for Army Training and Evaluation Program. He formed a convoy, and we rolled up the interstate to a Dahlonega Ranger training site for a whole week. All of us were angry with SSG Travis. Ft. Mac is a garrison post, but Travis came from a post that went to the field constantly for combat training. Thank God he scratched that itch he had and left us alone after that.

Dr. William Holmes Borders came to speak at the post chapel one day in 1983, and the choir was asked to sing. It was Black history month. He spoke so eloquently, and he didn't bite his tongue. I started visiting the Wheat Street Baptist Church where he pastored, right down the street from the famous Ebenezer Baptist Church. Occasionally, Vanessa and I would worship at Ebenezer. We would visit Dr. Martin Luther King Jr.'s house and the Center for Social and Non-Violence. I bought King's speeches on cassettes and books he had written. I appreciated the Pentecostal style of C.O.P.E., but sometimes I felt that we were too heavenly minded and no earthly good. But I kept that to myself.

Elder Franklin was genuine just like Evangelist Brown. He was a powerful preacher, and we are good friends to this day. One night at prayer meeting, one of our evangelists began prophesying in the spirit, and she stopped in front of me and declared that I was going to preach God's word. Well, I had already been teaching Sunday school, and I played some songs for the choir on the keyboard. But I wasn't so sure about preaching. I didn't give much thought to that pronouncement. At Ft. Mac people were receiving orders to go overseas all the time, but I felt lucky that my number hadn't been called. Life was just fine where I was, and I still hadn't gotten over the fear of flying. No. This was it. I was saving money, and in two years I was going to leave the military life. At least that was my plan.

Italy

But I did receive orders to go to Italy. It seemed that life in the military was like a roller coaster ride, with highs and lows. I prayed about it. And I had a powerful dream. I was on a plane that landed on a dark air strip. I got off the plane and started walking with my suitcase and duffel bag. As I walked, I came into a town with high rise apartments. There were people hanging out the window calling down to others on the street. There were cars, and honking horns. I took that to mean that I should go on to Italy and not worry about a thing.

When I arrived in Italy in 1984, I saw and heard the same kind of images and sounds that I experienced in my dreams. The Italian people used hand gestures, and they communicated to each other in a sometimes-loud voice, but it doesn't mean they are angry with each other. That is their culture. When I got off the plane and was dropped off at the train station, I kept hearing "Sciopero oggi!" Someone told me in broken English the train is on strike today. On strike? I'm supposed to be at Camp Darby in Livorno (Leghorn) before 8 p.m. The cab drivers were waving to people to take their cabs. I had no idea how far away Livorno was from Rome, so I hopped in a cab and showed the driver my destination. He smiled and said "Si!" We went down meandering roads, passed farms, through small villages, and over long bridges. I wondered if we had taken the scenic route.

When we finally arrived at Camp Darby, the driver was trying to explain to me that I owed him $300. I only had a hundred. He motioned for the Carabinieri (Italian Para-Military Police) to come over with an MP. They explained how much I owed. But I didn't have the money. The Americans were laughing at me for taking a cab all the way from Rome. In fact, I became the laughingstock of the whole base. A kind Staff Sergeant from the NCO club fronted me $200 dollars to pay the cab driver. But all during in-processing, people were asking me "Are you the nut who took a cab all the way from Rome to Livorno?" It took me a while to live that down.

Once I was acclimated into the 500th MP Company, I began making new friends. Of course they teased me about the cab ride, but overall, they were sympathetic. A couple of guys showed me around the post, and pointed out the PX, theatre, snack bar, mess hall, etc. I was sent on patrol with a tom-boyish, twenty-seven-year-old sergeant named Ersaline Blanks. She came from Pine Bluff, Arkansas. We became best friends instantly. In uniform she was slim and muscular. She could do push-ups and run just as good as any man, and she was very intelligent. I learned later that like me she grew up attending a Baptist church and even sang in a choir. We got along just fine. We drove down the street to the Carabinieri Casern adjoined to the post to pick up a Carabinieri. A curly headed Carabinieri dressed in a tan uniform, with a white strap across his chest got into the mint green Dodge Reliant, and we headed off post. We turned left and then left again and drove down Via Mediterranean. It led directly to the Mediterranean Ocean. We went to the place on the beach designated for American soldiers and their families. One of my duties would be to check this area during security checks. We never had any problems there.

Sergeant Blanks drove me to the various housing complexes where American soldiers lived. Occasionally we had to respond to domestic disputes or car break-ins at these places. Finally, I would get to use my MP training in live settings. The Carabinieris went along on each ride to be a liaison between Americans and Italians. Sometimes we responded to traffic accidents involving Americans and Italians. We had an interpreter at the station for each shift. I learned to speak Italian well. Time spent with the interpreters allowed me the opportunity to develop my language skills.

Another part of our duties called for patrolling around bunkers where ammunition was stored. These igloos, as we called them, were triangular-shaped mounds in a wooded area adjoined to the post. There were rock roads crisscrossing the area that gave us access. We were required to check the seals of each door to make sure they had not been tampered with. Each check had to be logged in at the hour. I would always have a good book with me when I went on this patrol.

We drove the new Chevrolet Humvees or od green jeeps. By day there were engineers working in the area performing maintenance and other services, but after 5 p.m. we had to secure the area. Some people have said that some of the ordinances dropped on the Gulf of Sidra during President Reagan and Ghadaffy's spat came from Camp Darby. We never encountered any thievery attempts, or activity from terrorists. The Carabinieris carried oozies and they didn't play games. We had M16A1 assault rifles, and there were warning signs all around the perimeter. I found plenty of time to read between security checks.

Reading Books on the Black Struggle

Around 1985 I began reading books on Marcus Garvey, Frederick Douglass, Kwame Nkruma, Rev. Leon Sullivan, the Pan African Congress, and other books on the Black struggle. This was a whole new world for me. I read countless biographies of the likes of Mahatma Ghandi, Booker T. Washington, Malcolm X, W.E.B. Dubois, and many others. One day I ordered cassettes of Malcolm X's speeches through Jet magazine. When they arrived, I listened to each one carefully. Malcolm contrasted the Berlin Conference with the Bang Dung Conference. I had never had this part of history explained to me in this way. I went to the library and found books on these subjects. I was gradually becoming political without even realizing it. Prior to leaving Atlanta for Italy, I had attended one of Jesse Jackson's campaign rallies at Piedmont Park. It was electrifying. Jesse's words were so prophetic and revealing. He exposed the hidden racism in Reagan's agenda with great clarity. But I feared he also intensified the rage of the white American males.

There was a white backlash to the Jimmy Carter presidency that I was starting to conceptualize. Carter, who was close friends with Dr. King's widow Mrs. Coretta King, had appointed Andrew Young to be U.N. ambassador, and Andy was involved with helping to broker a deal with the black majority and white minority in Rhodesia. Eventually the name was changed back to Zimbabwe and the black majority gained their independence. From what I could gather, this was the American Black Power movement connected with our brothers and sisters on the Continent. Rev. Leon Sullivan, a top General Motors leader, had introduced the "Sullivan Principles," calling for American corporations to divest in apartheid South Africa. Reagan was pushing his "Constructive Engagement" policies which meant, do nothing basically that would weaken the white power structure there.

I had been reading about imprisoned Nelson Mandela and Pan Africanist Steve Biko who was assassinated by the whites in South Africa. Now I was seeing the magnitude of white supremacy at home and abroad. In the military I had learned that of the 400+ generals only around 16 were black, and if Reagan could have his way, there would be even fewer. I could feel the climate in the military changing by the beginning of Reagan's second term. Just as I was beginning my tour in Italy, I couldn't relate my concerns to my fellow African Americans serving with me there. Ersaline, a fellow Arkansan, had seen racism up close as a little girl, but military life had altered her perspective on things. Racism was not a major problem for her now, nor for the other black service members. The same was not true for some of the Air Force men and women attached to Camp Darby. One black airman I encountered expressed outrage over the racist attitudes he was encountering in his ranks. All I could do for him was to be a sounding board.

Ersaline introduced me to an airman named Dennis. He and other airmen, women, and their families had started a Wednesday night Bible study at the fellowship hall in the Post Chapel. The Chapel was used by both Protestants and Catholics. We gathered there each Wednesday night with prayer, the reading of scriptures, and a hymn. Donuts and juice were served afterwards. Dennis and his wife were devout followers of Jesus Christ, and so were the others. There was one white airman there named Doug along with his wife and son. I learned later that he was a member of the Assembly of God church. They all leaned toward the Pentecostal tradition, like Evangelist Brown back in Germany.

I sat at the piano after one of these meetings and started playing some gospel tunes and soon members came over and started singing along. We had such a wonderful time that I was asked to play again at the next meeting, and the next, until it was added on. I played some of Andre Crouch's songs, and standard hymns familiar to the white members. Before we knew it, we had an integrated choir. Chaplain Donald Crippen from Alabama got wind of it and asked us to be his guests at Sundays' protestant service. We did, and it livened up the service so that the attendance increased. This meant so much to Chaplain Crippen, because now he had more people to preach to. Mrs. Crippen had a lovely voice. She and I would team up some Sundays and do a duet before her husband preached. They had two beautiful daughters who watched as their mother, and I learned new songs. I loved the Crippen family, and they showed me so much kindness. It's one thing to read about Christian character in the New Testament, but it is quite another thing to encounter it in real life.

Dennis was not a preacher, but he was versed in the scriptures, and he was upright in character. Chaplain Crippen was a proud Methodist. He didn't put a lot of emotion into his preaching the way some black folks were used to. He was aware of the slight disconnect, however. Some of the members were anxious for a different kind of church service, one that involved the movement of the Holy Spirit, prayer, and the laying of hands. I explained to the choir that I had been called to preach prior to leaving Atlanta. In fact, Elder Franklin had allowed me to bring the word on a few Sundays. Sermons came to me all the time as I read the Bible.

I felt strongly that I was being called into the ministry. And given all that I had been through, who was to say that God had not orchestrated things so that now His plan was being made manifest. After one of our Wednesday night meetings, we agreed to hold church services on Sunday in the Post Chapel following the Protestant church service at 12:30 p.m. Doug invited an Assembly of God pastor he knew from Vicenza, Italy to preach for us. The white pastor came, and he preached with great authority and conviction. We were all encouraged and inspired by his preaching. We took up an offering to help him with travel expenses until we could make financial arrangements to bring him back weekly. A meeting between the pastor, his wife, and Doug seemed cliquish. Following one such meeting, we were told that we would have to raise more money if the pastor was going to keep driving from Vicenza. The suspicion kept building until the weak arrangement with the pastor collapsed. By then Doug and his wife were having serious marital problems, and his wife wanted to return to the U.S. I tried to encourage them both, but she had made up her mind. It was a terrible break up. Dennis and other core members received assignment orders which meant returning to the U.S. Dennis and his family went to Lackland AF base in San Antonio.

We kept the Bible study going. I sent a letter to Elder Franklin explaining to him our situation. He had been planning to ordain me, but I left before he had the chance, so he convened the other ministers of the church, and they agreed to send me my license and ordination papers to preach. Chaplain Donald Crippen signed off on the necessary paperwork for me to serve under him as lay leader. He gave me plenty of his old books from seminary to help deal with marriage counseling, church administration, handling the sacraments, and other things that I had not learned at C.O.P.E. Crippen said something to me one day that hit me like a ton of bricks. He said, "You know Joe, one of the things that hurt black preachers is their lack of education." The look on his face when he said this spoke volumes. Taking on the responsibility of running a church presented to me great challenges.

I realized that I needed more schooling. The Army was also challenging soldiers to have at least a 100 score on their General Technical (GT) test. This test measures one's word knowledge, mathematical skills, paragraph comprehension, and mechanical comprehension. I had a 99, so I started taking classes. By now, Vanessa and Aundria had joined me in Italy. We were staying at an apartment in a beautiful village called Collesalvetti. The Comandante, or Commander of the Carabinieri at Camp Darby, lived across the street from us. We greeted each other often. I had other Italian friends in the neighborhood also.

Vanessa and I had met a Ugandan woman named Marcheline who was married to a very kind Italian doctor. They lived in a house built in the thirteenth century on the top of a ridge. We were invited there for dinner on numerous occasions. I can still taste the great quality of the Chianti red wine produced right on the property. Marcheline was street smart and very savvy. She would drive all over Italy. Our favorite eating spot about three miles from our home was a little hole in the wall, but it stayed packed with customers. I was addicted to their spaghetti carbonara with the aged, tangy, bacon. I've never tasted a dish that could come close to their version. I don't recall the name of the place.

I started reading up on Italian history, mainly the part that led to U.S. involvement. I read about Benito Mussolini in WWII. El Duce tried to emulate Hitler.

He himself had imperialist ambitions. Under him the Italians sought to colonize Ethiopia in 1935 but failed. I met many people from Ethiopia and Eritrea in Italy. I learned that Eritrea teamed up with Italy to overthrow Ethiopia. Malcolm X was right when he said that history is that subject that best rewards all research. I studied a little about medieval Europe, and the Medici family who are credited with starting financial institutions. Vanessa, Aundria, and I went to Venice where the Medici family was said to have come. We rode into the city on a train just in time to see the red sun dancing on the water. We visited certain ancient buildings and churches. We ate at the tourist restaurants which were ordinary compared to the ones off the beaten pathway around Livorno.

We also traveled to Bologna, Florence, Milan, and Rome. One of our favorite spots was Viareggio. We were there one weekend on a marriage retreat arranged by the Provost Marshal Maj. Boone. During a recess, I stepped onto the balcony overlooking the market square. I was dressed in an Italian suit and a tan trench coat. I was casually looking over the market when I noticed a crowd gathering beneath the balcony. They were all looking up at me as if something was wrong. After a while a young man called out in broken English and said, "Eh man, voi Billy Dee William?" I started laughing and said back to him in Italian "No soldato Americano io!" In English I said, "No. I am an American soldier." They all started laughing. Many rich and famous people from America flock to this beautiful resort. Vanessa,

Aundria, and I loved the open markets and seafood restaurants. Everywhere we went the older Italian women would squeeze my daughter's cheeks and say "molta Bella!" which meant very beautiful. Aundria basked in their attention.

Aundria attended the Department of Defense elementary school at Camp Darby. I would occasionally stop in and check on her progress. She learned to speak Italian words as she made friends with the other kids. She would spend the night with a black girl named Chiquita. They were the best of friends. Her mother attended church with us. Her father had a problem with alcoholism. One night he was driving under the influence and lost control of his car. I'm told he struck a tree, and Chiquita went through the front windshield and died. Her little brother was in the car as well. He suffered multiple fractures. I was not on duty that night, but Vanessa and I visited the son and father in the Italian hospital. Neither of them were wearing seatbelts. It was a great tragedy for the family, community, and Aundria. A dear friend of mine who served as a minister under my leadership lost his wife to a traffic accident not long after. That was one MP duty that I dreaded performing. I handled accidents, but none were fatal.

I tried to polish up on my Robert Rules of Order so I could conduct church meetings now that I had to handle finances and lead the church in decision making. We appointed a treasurer, secretary, deacons, and an assistant minister who was Min. Gloria

Jackson. We were a motley crew from different denominational backgrounds, so having a female minister in the pulpit didn't sit right with some. I pointed out to them in the Bible where women had always exercised leadership positions among believers. There were other small issues that arose from time to time. I could write to Elder Franklin to get answers, or I called on my good friend Chaplain Crippen. My main priority was preparing the sermons for Sunday and helping others to develop their spiritual gifts. I played for the choir, sang, and pastored. At the time it was both rewarding and challenging. I had to balance my MP duties with church duties. Sometimes I would come to Bible study and choir rehearsal wearing my badge and .45 pistol the whole time.

School was going fine also. Vanessa and I decided that we would both pursue our high school diploma. I had a GED, but a high school diploma would allow me to take college courses at the University of Maryland satellite campus at Darby. During my studies to raise my GT score I met a wonderful Bostonian named Mr. Brown. He had a Boston accent that we all made fun of. But through his humor and commitment he inspired me, other soldiers, and family members to learn. He simplified mathematical formulas for us in such a way that even trigonometry became simple. Vanessa also took classes from him. She and I would stay up late at night working out math problems and going over history and English concepts.

Vanessa and I passed the exam and received our high school diplomas. We felt so proud of ourselves. We couldn't thank Mr. Brown enough as well as the other teachers who helped us. I continued my education by enrolling in the University of Maryland and began taking courses. Of the four courses I took, my scores were A's, B, and one C+ in English. My confidence level went through the roof. Now I was set on an academic journey. I was not going to stop until I got my master's degree. Because I was able to raise my GT score to 110, I now qualified for Officer Candidate School or OCS. This would have made me a commissioned officer in the military. I thought about registering for the school on a few occasions.

Meanwhile, the church was running smoothly. The choir sounded good. One day I was approached by the post deputy commander, Lt. Col Hardin. He asked me if the choir could perform for the annual Italian American banquet. He said we would only need to sing two songs. I told him yes and asked the choir to get ready. There was a young white guy playing drums for us; unfortunately, I can't remember his name. But like me he was acquiring the skill. A certain young soldier named Cheryl sang with us with her beautiful soprano.

John Evans from Atlanta, Ersaline Blanks, Vernon Taylor, and about twelve others were with us at the banquet. God's Got it All in Control by Shirley Caesar was our first number. And then I sang Jesus is Love by the Commodores. The room was still as I sang until

I started climbing, and then there were outbursts of handclapping. When I came to the end of the songs all I heard was "Ripetitivo! Ripetitivo!" Col. Hardin rushed over to me and asked me if I would sing it again, so I did. And the same thing happened at the end, so I sang the song a third time. Not long after that event, Col. Hardin presented me with a certificate of appreciation, and he became a dear friend.

Major Shackleford and his wife and daughter would attend church service with us every now and then. He and his family also loved listening to the choir. His daughter wanted me to give her piano lessons. But I wasn't that versed in music. Maj. Shackleford had an idea of telling the story about black achievement during Black History Month. He enlisted my choir, and other soldiers to do some reading while he narrated the whole event. It went very well. Chaplain Crippen, who was in attendance, stood up and declared that he had learned something about black folks he never knew. I think we all did. Maj. Shackleford was a scholarly black officer, who walked with his head held high. He was very perceptive about the changes that were happening under President Reagan. In fact, he and another black captain, Captain Echols, had confided in me about some problems they were having with their overdue promotions and being slighted at staff meetings.

Discrimination was showing itself boldly around this time. Even a black chaplain assistant under the Catholic chaplain complained to me about being called a nigger by his Catholic boss. Reagan made it fashionable to be racist again. I had been selected to be desk sergeant at the MP station following my promotion to sergeant. I was allowed to place my weapon in a safe at the station on Sundays when I was scheduled to preach. The operation sergeant and the Provost Marshal, Major Boone, were alright with this arrangement. One day I reported for duty at the desk, and I noticed a flyer on the bulletin board. It had a white fist against the backdrop of a U.S. flag. There was no doubt in my mind what it stood for, which is white power. I asked Sergeant Stratton, whom I was relieving, who put the flyer on that board. He shrugged as if he didn't know. I had been noticing the jealousy from some of my white peers after my promotion and other accolades. SP4 Connally who had served with me at Ft. Mac was spreading rumors saying that I was so religious at Ft. Mac that I refused to carry a weapon. I had to confront him about the lie one day.

My squad leader Sergeant Campbell repeated that rumor. This Tennessean redneck needed someone to look down on given that he had been in the Army above twelve years and he was still a buck sergeant. He and his wife had no children, only a little dog. He treated me nice during my first two years in Country, but Reaganism was setting in and it now seemed like he was trying to make my life pure hell. He was over me in position, but not rank. He was constantly trying to find something for which to write me up. I had about four months left on my tour of service at which time I was leaving the military, so all I had to do was put up with his crap for a little while longer. Major Shackleford called on me again. This time he was in a dilemma. He had invited a black two-star general to speak at the Dr. Martin Luther King, Jr. Holiday Commemorative service. He had heard me speak at the church and felt that I could fill in for the general. Major Shackleford and I had many in-depth discussions about Reagan and the struggle of black folks. But what he had in mind was a feel-good talk for about six minutes. I thought about it, but I had to be true to myself and those courageous black leaders I had read about in history. I was not the same Joseph that came to Italy in 1984. It was now 1987 and I understood things a little better. I had read much of Dr. King's writings and I had listened to his speeches. I was not going to speak in honor of so great a man with a nice little sermonette. The message that I would deliver had to have substance and relevance to what was happening around us.

I had only three days to prepare. I thought about the resolutions people make when they are sitting in a church listening to powerful words of conviction. Only to return to their old routine after they leave the church. I said that's what America has done, since the death of Dr. King. The nation was trying to do the right thing even under President Jimmy Carter, but racism had reared its ugly head again. And America, like the Bible's proverbial dog, had returned to its own vomit. When I finished speaking, most of the people in the chapel stood up and clapped. But our post commander, Col. Nadowski sat on the front pew staring at me as if I had committed treason. Major Shackelford gave the benediction and then came over to shake my hand and to tell me what a powerful message I had delivered.

Lt. Col Hardin came over and shook my hand. Other enlisted persons from my company came up and shook my hand. Some patted me on the back and praised me for being so eloquent. But the next day I received a note. I was to report to my company commander, Captain Baker immediately. I went into his office, saluted him, and he said, "At ease!" He asked me "What do you preach at your church service?" I told him I spoke about Christ and his crucifixion. He said he would like to attend my church soon. I told him he was welcome to come any Sunday. He asked me how often I visited Major Shackleford's house. I told him I had been to his house for dinner a few times. He said, "That's all. You are dismissed." I saluted and left, knowing full well I was under investigation by the post commander himself. They must have thought I had been radicalized by some black militant organization or something. But the truth of the matter was, I had awoken from all the reading I had done.

The next three weeks were hell. Some mornings I didn't want to get out of bed to face the onslaught of hate and attempts to discredit me. I didn't know what to expect next. Major Shackleford had his own challenges. I couldn't confide in him. So I went to my old friend, the one who helped me when I was at my lowest point in Germany. I called on God. After a long heartfelt prayer, I felt kind of rejuvenated. I asked God to either remove me or remove my enemies. I walked back into the lion den (the MP station) and carried out my duties as before. Even the Operation sergeant was acting differently now. First Sergeant Ragsdale knew nothing about what I was going through; neither was he aware of the racist activity going on in the ranks. He was a good-natured white gentleman, and a professional soldier. He sent a memo to all the sergeants, of which I was one, saying the whole company was to assemble in formation for a company photo, and there was to be no horse playing at the photo shoot. We assembled that evening around 4 p.m. dressed in our class A uniforms. Sergeant Campbell, who was short, was in the front row at the end. He stood grinning like a Cheshire cat with his middle finger sticking out when the camera flashed. A week later the First Sergeant summoned all the NCOs to his office. He asked us if we had heard him say there was to be no horse playing for the company photo. We all replied yes. He said, well, I need a statement from each of you to that effect. We completed the statements, and the First Sergeant showed us the photo with Sgt. Campbell displaying his middle finger. Later Campbell received an Article 15, which deducts money from a soldier's pay and is recorded into his personnel file as punishment for a violation. He was also removed from being my squad leader.

Captain Baker received orders to return to the U.S. for another assignment. He had a short time to process out; meanwhile, Col. Nadowski came under scrutiny by the Inspector General (I.G.) for misappropriating government funds. It turns out that the Post Commander had a love for baseball, so he diverted funds to spruce up the baseball field. He was relieved of his post. If I hadn't seen it with my own eyes, no one could have convinced me that a miracle had just taken place. All three of my adversaries had been moved just as I had requested God to do. My faith in God was strengthened, and I had a renewed boldness to preach and get involved with the struggle for justice.

I knew I was too radical for the Army, so there was no question about re-enlisting for another 3 years. I was going to leave the Army and join some civil rights organization to further the work of those leaders I had been reading about. I would need more credentials, so going to college was on the top of my list. I had been saving up money through the Veteran Education Assistant Program or VEAP. I had saved $8,000 when I left the Army. The program matched $3 for every $1 a soldier put in. It was a great return on my investment. Vanessa, Aundria, and I flew to Ft. Dix, New Jersey to process out, and then we took a Greyhound bus to Atlanta. In Atlanta we moved in with Mary Lee, my sister-in-law, her husband Michael, and Michael Jr. I went to West Helena to retrieve my 1978 Grand Prix. Aunt Vannie had kept it for me for three years.

I had $5,000 in the bank to tie me over until I found a job. I went to Swift Meat Packing Co. and was offered a temporary position until the vacationing workers returned. I said thanks but no thanks. I thought that surely my MP resume would impress the top leaders at the Army Air Force Exchange Service (AAFES) at Ft. Gillem because I had dispatched MP patrol officers to the various warehouses to investigate larcenies and petty car break-ins. I also handled some of the cases. I went to the personnel office and applied. I got a call from them saying my application had been accepted. They started me off with $5.50 an hour, which was not bad in 1987. I worked the night shift. Nights were when AAFES were losing the greatest amount of merchandise to theft. There were four warehouses that had the greatest theft activity. I would walk through and get acquainted with the workers, most of whom were black. We would laugh and joke about things. I knew some were genuine and others were sizing me up. I prayed one night and asked God to let me see the ones that were stealing the merchandise. I dressed in my old Army camouflage uniform one night and took up a position behind a tire well of one of the eighteen wheelers. I could see the dock where the workers were loading and unloading merchandise. Soon a worker jumped off the loading dock, and another worker handed him several boxes. He ran past me to his car in the parking lot and went back to the dock. I waited to see if there would be more activity. There was none, so I called for the MPs and other AAFES security officers to meet me at the parking lot. I posted them by the car, while the MP and I went to the warehouse to arrest the suspects. I wrote out a statement and gave it to the MP, and a copy to the supervisor. We saved AAFES around $5000 that night. I went to the other warehouses and did the same.

I was called into the office the next morning and awarded a check for $300. Another time the check was $500, and they kept getting higher. Next, I was given a raise. The top officials of AAFES security said they hadn't been able to catch that many thieves in its history. One top ranking official wanted to take a ride with me to see how I was so effective. I told him I prayed about it, but that went over his head. Surely, I possessed some type of superior police skills. I did not. These crooks weren't very smart.

One night, I was surveilling the loading dock at Building 305 when a tall black man jumped off the dock carrying a brown box. He went to his car and placed the box in his trunk and went back into the building. I had spoken to him earlier. He was a man in his early sixties, clean shaven, and dressed neatly. I went in to confront him. I pulled him aside and said to him "I saw you put AAFES's merchandise in your trunk." Tears began to well up in his eyes. He said "Please brother. Don't turn me in. I just got out of the pen. I'm on probation." I had already called for AAFES security backup. A part of me said show no mercy because he should know better, and another side of me was saying what if he is right? Did I want to be responsible for sending a brother back to penitentiary for years. I scolded him and told him to return the merchandise. He went to his car and retrieved the box and brought it to me. I took it to his supervisor. And I looked at the old man. He dropped his head. I met my backup at the entrance and told them everything was alright. I felt conflicted that night when I went home. I shared the incident with Vanessa. But she didn't have any critique for me.

I ran into Clarence, my old MP Operation Sergeant from FT. Mac. We were at the Postal Credit Union in Hapeville. He told me to be sure and register to take the postal examine before my 90 days expired. He said that I would automatically receive 10 points just for being a veteran. He recommended I buy a postal workbook at the bookstore and complete all the practice exercises in the book. I followed his instructions and prayed for God's help. Chico Conde had served with me in Italy. He too needed a job, so I shared Clarence's advice with him. He told me that he left the Army with a less than honorable discharge. I said "So what? All they can do is turn you down!" and he said, 'You're right!" We both went to apply, and we both were accepted and given an exam date. We studied our books and passed the exam. We were so excited. I started working at the post office in Lakewood down Jonesboro Road near Forest Park, Georgia.

Chico became a postal supervisor in no time. He had always been very intelligent. I kept my night job with AAFES for a while. I wasn't ready to stop getting those bonus checks. The top officials had even offered me a promotion if I stayed. $7.50 an hour was good, but the Post Office offered me $10.50 an hour plus benefits so I chose the Post Office. I credit God's intervention with my success. I could clearly see that my white counterparts at AFFES were not more intelligent than me, but they had access. I felt sorry for some of my white colleagues when I learned that some didn't even have a high school diploma. They grew up there in Forest Park, Georgia. I felt a wind of jealousy when I received those bonus checks following each arrest. Having served as an MP, and trained in other areas, I did possess abilities that they lacked. I never slighted any of them and in fact, I tried to share my strategies with them.

Leaving AAFES in the mornings and delivering the mail by day took its toll on me. I eventually resigned from AAFES and focused on delivering the mail. Vanessa and I were able to get a VA loan to buy a house, so we did. The Grand Prix was stolen at a MARTA train station, so I bought a brand-new gray Pontiac Grand Am, my first new car. I enrolled at Beulah Heights Bible College on Berne Street in Atlanta in 1992. I commuted back and forth for evening classes after work. Prof. Samuel Chand and Dr. Keiller became my academic guardians for the next five years. I was glad to be back in the classroom studying. The professors would give us around 25 vocabulary words to learn every week. We discussed these words and became familiar with them. And we ran into all these words in the various courses we took. I am so grateful to this day for being made to learn these new words.

The professors at Beulah Heights are dedicated to educating men and women for the service of the body of Christ. Founded in 1918, it is a conservative university which posed a challenge to me at first, but I was able to navigate and find the sources that Dr. Martin Luther King Jr. had interacted with. All the reading I had been doing overseas exposed me to Reinhold Niebuhr, Walter Rauschenbusch, Ralph Waldo Emerson, and many others. These scholars were not front and center at Beulah Heights. Plato and Aristotle were mentioned in my Western Civilization class. But there was no in-depth discussion about their influence on Western society. I would have to learn that independently. The fact that Dr. King kept referring to these philosophers in his speeches suggested to me that I should give careful reflection to their writings. I would also seek out information about Socrates.

Beulah Heights College's library was very small and limited at this time. It had not become a university yet. It had a few books about the black struggle. Once, I stumbled upon a book by a black author, Leroy Banks, who was ridiculing Dr. Martin L. King Jr. for leading the bus boycott in Montgomery in the 50s. His argument was that preachers shouldn't get involved in politics. I thought to myself it was the white church leaders that Dr. King was confronting in his famous Letter from the Birmingham Jail. They were not only involved in politics, but the religious institutions they represented were strong supporters of Jim Crow. I wanted to throw the book into the trashcan, but it wasn't mine. It was then that I realized that unless something changed at Beulah, many black preachers coming through that college would be little good for social and political change in the black community. And as I visited black churches around Atlanta and the country, I could see the effects of conservative teaching on my fellow black religious leaders. This reality became amplified when I joined the NAACP around 1990.

It was around 1989 that I was reading about a Mr. James Jackson, president of the Clayton County NAACP. He was in the Clayton News Daily papers challenging injustices in the county. His arguments were sound, and he was courageous. Joining the local NAACP branch was definitely on my to do list, but for now I wanted to receive as much education as I could get. I had already begun reading books on the NAACP, and other black organizations. Rarely did a conversation arise in class about the black struggle. Beaulah Heights College was strictly religious almost to the fault of indoctrination. I couldn't allow myself to be indoctrinated. I had resisted it even in the military; yet, in the military I learned so much about America and its stated values. I also learned about its hypocrisies.

Strands of information about the black struggle would surface sometimes during my Beulah Heights experience. For instance, in my Movement of the Holy Spirit class we were examining the roots of the modern Pentecostal movement. We came to a chapter dealing with a black preacher and bible college student named William J. Seymour who had been studying in Texas under a White instructor named Charles Parham. Parham was teaching his students that speaking in tongues was the sign that one had received the Holy Spirit. Because of segregation, Seymour was made to sit in the hallway away from the white students. He truly believed Parham's theory, and so he began teaching it. Some church leaders closed their doors to him thinking that his doctrine was heretical. But he was invited to speak at a church in California. His teachings caused a ruckus there also, and he was locked out of that church. The woman who invited him offered to host him and his teachings at her house. He began teaching there until her house became overwhelmed with visitors. They found an old horse stable in an alley in Los Angeles in 1909. The Holy Spirit started moving in that place in such a mighty way that people started flocking there from around the world. Some tagged it the Azusa Street revival. The local papers at the time referred to it as "Nigger alley."

It is said that Charles H. Mason attended, and he too was baptized in the Spirit. He was one of the few people there who had been ordained. William J. Seymour had no desire to start a church denomination, but Mason did. He led the efforts to form the Church of God in Christ. Certain whites who came to him for ordination went to Pine Bluff, Arkansas to start the Assembly of God church. There it is. It is, as former President Jimmy Carter once said, in America race is never far below the surface. It is the elephant in the room that not many religious folks, black or white, care to discuss. Dr. King said frequently that the most segregated hour in America is 11:00 a.m. on Sunday. I remember how uncomfortable certain professors were when I would ask them to elaborate on racial matters in our lessons. They couldn't wait to move on. Even black characters in the Bible were glossed over. Some of my classmates would get stimulated from the brief discussions I would raise on the topic of race; others would be clearly annoyed.

Beulah Heights' student body was made up of people from at least 15 countries. I thought that was so neat. Through the course of my studies, I was elected student president around 1996. It was such a great honor. I had a vision of having a church service after the manner of the Book of Acts where the disciples came together on one accord and the Holy Spirit arrested them. They were speaking in different languages (Acts 2:6). At this church service all the students would participate in their own language and culture; afterwards, we would have a food tasting with cuisines reflecting each country. It was such an amazing worship setting. Neither white nor black Americans were allowed to dominate the service. I saw a freedom in the nationals that I had not seen in everyday class settings. They expressed a deep gratitude to me for having done this. I wanted to make it a reoccurring event.

I met wonderful people at Beaulah Heights, both Americans and foreigners. A Kenyan named Benson Karanja became one of my dearest friends. He went on to become president of Beulah Heights University. We used to have deep conversations about Jomo Kenyatta, and the Mau Mau revolution that led to Kenya's independence. We talked about the good and bad influences of tribalism. I remember him for his strong intellect. I met his wife and children also. I did what I could to help all the students enjoy a rich experience at Beulah. African Americans were gradually becoming the greatest percentage of the student body. Even Bishop Eddie Long would come back for refresher courses, and his church, New Birth Missionary Baptist Church, hosted our graduation ceremonies.

While I attended Beulah Heights, I continued to worship at C.O.P.E with Elder Franklin on Campbelltown Road. He too had attended Beulah Heights. He placed me over the Evangelistic Program at the church in 1988. I would lead teams of members into the surrounding neighborhoods to witness, going door to door. We went to Creekside housing project on Stanton Road about three minutes from the church. Some members of our church lived there, and before long we were having church service with live music and good food on some Saturday afternoons. Some of the young children would come mainly for the food. Others enjoyed hearing me sing Jesus is Love by the Commodores as well as the other beautiful singers.

When summer was in full swing in 1989, I organized baseball games for the youths. I gave them money for their report cards when they had good grades. At the baseball games we gave them hotdogs and hamburgers with juices or sodas. I taught them the virtues of education and working for what they wanted in life. There was a 15-year-old teenager who kept having run-ins with the police. Some of the other kids told me about the stolen gun he was carrying. I pulled him and the other young boys together and told them my story about getting kicked out of school and joining the Army. They listened in disbelief. Even the one with the gun confided in me. I told him how I felt growing up without a father, and why I acted out in school. He listened for a while, but one day he was arrested for stealing a car. The other kids broke the news about it at our next baseball game.

I went to Councilman Heckstall in East Point in the summer of 1989 and told him I needed some jobs for the older boys and girls that were in my charge. He agreed to help me. We approached certain fast-food restaurants in the area and received commitments to hire some of the young people. This was great news and progress. Evangelism for me was not only about salvation; it was about helping people get out of housing projects, and away from a life of poverty and crime. I wanted to enlighten these children and expose them to greater Atlanta, and new possibilities.

On February 11, 1990, Nelson Mandela was released from prison in South Africa. He was scheduled to tour the U.S. I had gotten word one day that he would be at Phillips Arena. I went to Elder Franklin and told him I wanted to use the church van to take the children to see Mr. Mandela and witness history. This was in 1990. I loaded them up and we went to see Mr. Mandela. It was strange to some of the children, but for me it was a great celebration. I was seeing my hero in living color. For me and people around the world, he was a living legend and a man of great character and courage. He came out amid chants and applause and stood there in the glistening sunlight unbowed and unbroken. His words were certain, seasoned with goodwill toward all. I think it did more for me than the children. He was surrounded by local and national dignitaries as he made his remarks, and then he raised his fist up high and led the chant "Amandla!" the crowd responded "Gwetoo!" which means Power to the People! It was a glorious day.

By now I had joined the Clayton County NAACP branch. I would attend the monthly meetings and even serve on the committees. Oscar Blalock and other gentlemen served on the powerful legal redress committee. They handled cases involving the police and racist convictions of black people in the county. We received many of these types of complaints at the time. Mr. James Jackson had died, and Mr. Ben

Marsh had succeeded him. Ben Marsh had been a major in the Army. He was very polished and soft spoken, but also very effective. He knew how to build a consensus and lead the branch into action. One day he appointed me to chair the membership committee. I took my job very seriously. I went around to the various black churches and conducted a membership drive.

Our membership grew steadily. This was a time when the black people of Clayton County really saw the need for the NAACP, which made my job easier. The branch enjoyed strong support from the leading black preachers in the county also. Reverends Charles Grant, Hopie Strickland, Homer Pitman, Barron Banks, W.C. Smith, Arthur Powell, Dr. Cornelius Henderson, and Dr. John D. Waters were towering figures in the branch. Both the executive committee meetings and the branch meetings were solemn events. We opened with a word of prayer followed by the adoption of the agenda and the reading of the minutes. Next, we moved down each agenda item.

I learned that the branch had been enacted in 1986. Some of the chartered members were James Jackson (1948-1990) president, his wife Johnny N. Jackson, Wade Starr-1st Vice president, Oscar Blalock, Eula Ponds Perry Secretary, Frenda Norwood, John Trotter, the only white guy, Rev. McCalister Hollins and wife Cynthia Hollins, Rev. Charles Grant, John Brooks executive secretary, Carolyn and Gail Davenport, and Reda Brooks. Our numbers were strong with 119 people pledging their support to start the new branch. On October 18, 1986, the Clayton County branch of the NAACP was chartered. The Jacksons had an extensive record of civil rights involvement that stemmed back to Tugaloo College in Mississippi. They enrolled in the college a year after the deaths of three civil rights workers Andrew Goodman, James Chaney, and Michael Schwerner in 1964.

The Jacksons were exposed to numerous civil rights leaders at Tugaloo including Dr. Martin L. King Jr., and Fannie Lou Hamer. There were civil rights rallies and planning sessions conducted there all the time. They arrived in Clayton County Georgia in 1979. James, a mathematician major and financial auditor, was hoping to settle down and live a modest life, but he was approached by Wade and other leaders who felt that Clayton County needed a strong Black organization to tackle some of the major inequities they faced in the county. There were several choices and models to choose from, i.e., Southern Christian Leadership Conference (SCLC), Urban League, the NAACP, or civic league. They chose the NAACP, and Mr. Jackson became its first president. They hit the ground running. The first major item on the agenda was to get more black teachers and principals hired. Their efforts were met with stiff resistance by the white power structure. But over a short period of time white leaders knew that they had a foe to be reckoned with. Jackson and branch leaders established a strong network with the black clergies and prominent churches in the county from which to draw membership and financial support for the new branch. The Black intelligentsia was well represented in the branch. Jackson and his colleagues insisted that NAACP policies be followed as they molded the branch into a sound and potent organization. Maintaining the budget was a constant challenge.

In 1987 amid their challenges in Clayton County, the NAACP leaders were called on by civil rights veteran, the Hon. Rev. Hosea Williams, to come and protest with them in Forsyth County about 50 miles outside of Atlanta. Hosea Williams had presented a document to the Forsyth County Sheriff offering forgiveness by blacks for the 1912 expulsion of black folks from the county after an 18-year-old black man was accused of raping and murdering a white woman. Williams was seeking to negotiate the return of Black residents and black businesses. The protests were met with rocks and bottles as the white citizens began pelting them and calling them "niggers" from behind the police barricade. So much for a life of modesty, the Jacksons were back in the struggle. He would go on to tackle many issues in Clayton County.

By his third term as president, his sickness took its toll on him. James Jackson died in 1990 of complications from Hodgkin's disease. Clayton County lost a warrior for justice. I would read his statements in the local paper as he articulated the issues. I was looking forward to joining the NAACP, but I kept procrastinating as I was involved with my church. I joined the branch immediately after Jackson's death. The spirit of James Jackson loomed largely at the NAACP meetings I attended. It was well organized. The erudite Dr. Eddie White didn't hesitate to correct someone who was not in line with Robert's Rules of Order which is the standard parliamentary procedures used in the United States. Once the branch membership decided on a course of action it was then executed by the president, vice president and committee members.

One day in 1991, I accompanied Rev. Barron Banks, Ben Marsh, Wade Starr, and Oscar Blalock to a meeting with Clayton County School superintendent and other board members. At issue was the under representation of black teachers and principals at the schools. The Rev. Banks, a Presbyterian minister, had the courage and the eloquence of a Jesse Jackson. Mr. Ben Marsh presented the case before Superintendent Lovin, who flat out rejected our proposal. After negotiating back and forth over the matter, Rev. Banks stood up and threw up both of his hands signaling the meeting was over. We all stood and walked out in protest. Our white counterparts did not know what to expect next, but they knew there would have to be some type of compromise. Meanwhile, the legal redress committee had been at the police station confronting Chief Ronnie Thorton about the under representation of black police officers in the county. The erudite Dr. Glen Dowell led the negotiations there, and he prevailed. Dowell was known for his signature bowties. You would have thought he was a member of the Nation of Islam. I don't recall him ever losing a political debate. It was around 1990 when the NAACP branch office at 699 Roundtree Road was bombed. I don't believe anyone was in the office. It had been bombed before, which was why I never sat with my back to the door during meetings. Clayton County had a reputation for being a hot bed for KKK. Their members used to give out leaflets at the intersection of Hwy 138 and Jonesboro Road. Jonesboro is the county seat, and there is a large, manicured, Confederate cemetery not far from the landmark train depot. Confederate symbols dotted downtown Jonesboro to welcome all visitors. This is Gone with the Wind country. The old ax-wielding former Gov. Lester Maddox owned an estate about 10 miles down Tara Blvd.

Prior to 1986 when the Clayton County NAACP was founded, many black Atlantans didn't care to drive through Clayton County because of undue harassment by the police. Fayetteville, the next town over, was just as bad. I was about to get an up-close look at Jim Crow and all its intricacies. It turns out that the culprits behind the bombings were white teens. District Attorney Bob Keller said they were just playing a prank. The NAACP leaders settled the matter with Keller and avoided jail time for the youths, but some type of punishment and fines were meted out.

Keller owed us one, and I didn't forget that. The Clayton County School Board eventually bowed to our pressure and hired three black principals and more black teachers. The branch leaders were effective. Our 1st VP Wade Starr and John Trotter came up with a brilliant idea to start a newsletter to circulate among the black community. This accomplished two major things. One, it allowed the NAACP to control its narrative and, two, we would be able select the best white political candidate who would support our interests. We couldn't endorse candidates because of our 501 (C 3) status, so we had to be very clever when communicating with our constituents. I would simply stand in the pulpit at various churches and talk about the shortcomings and outright neglect of specific candidates and extoll the virtues of their opponents. Most people knew what I meant.

Wade Starr is a genius, and a political maverick. He always stayed a step ahead of all of us. I was never into politics. My field has always been civil and human rights, so I tried to stay in my lane. Ben Marsh decided not to run for another term as our president. We hated to see him go. At our annual Freedom Fund Gala of 1991, he awarded me a plaque for significantly increasing our membership. Under his leadership, the branch had accomplished amazing things. Our financial house was in order, and we enjoyed great support from both blacks and whites in the county. We had several white life members of our branch. Many believed in the work we were doing, and some simply wanted to keep their enemies close to them. Marsh was a true diplomat, and a skillful administrator. He was succeeded by Mr. Oscar Blalock, and Mrs. Efuma Oukadike became VP. They continued in the direction we were on. I continued as membership chair. We had a strong youth council of which my daughter Aundria Latrice Wheeler and my niece Patonya Price were members. We would go to the various NAACP state and regional conventions, and we learned a lot. I had read up on one-time CEO Roy Wilkins, and Dr. Ben Hooks. I became friends with our regional director, the powerful Earl T. Shinholster (1950-2000), and our state president Mr. Walter C. Butler II. Mr. Shinholster had been advising the governor and influencing the passage of laws for the state of Georgia. I would see him on the evening news articulating issues as an authority when I was stationed at Ft. McPherson. Sometimes he dressed in African attire. We started calling him Brother Earl the way the previous generation called Malcolm X Brother Malcolm. Shinholster had served as 5th Regional Director 17 years before going off to serve as Acting president and CEO of the NAACP in Baltimore, Maryland around the beginning of 1995.

Mr. Shinholster was a true servant-leader. He cared deeply about black people, and he earned the respect of white leaders, black leaders, and his peers alike. He took the reins at the National Office when Mr. Ben Chavis got caught in a scandal in which he misappropriated NAACP funds to settle a sexual harassment lawsuit. Brother Earl was a steady hand at the helm of the NAACP until former Congressman Kweisi Mfume (D-Md.) was awarded the position of president and CEO. Many of us were saddened that Brother Earl was passed over for the position. He was organic, the real NAACP, we thought. We felt that Mr. Mfume was just a name brand.

I remember attending my first 5th regional convention at Hilton Head, SC around 1995. We were at the Marriott Hotel, and it was a great convention. I learned a lot about the association. We assembled for lunch in the banquet hall waiting for the head table guests to arrive. Some had started eating already. Brother Earl walked to the podium and said very politely "Brothers and sisters I see some of you have already begun eating but pause a minute while the minister says grace." After grace he said, "Enjoy your meal." He said it with so much grace, dignity, and genuine love for our people. I determined that day that I would be that kind of a leader also.

Brother Earl always treated us as if we were the most important people in the room. He was so knowledgeable about Black history, American history, and world history. And he wasn't arrogant about it. I loved him. I was with him at the Georgia State NAACP conference banquet at the World Congress Center around June 10, 2000, just before he was killed. He had been traveling down Interstate 85 south toward Montgomery with an African delegation. I am told they were in a Ford Explorer when a tire blew out. The driver lost control of the vehicle. I am still suspicious about the accident. I was devastated the next day when I got the news. Shinholster had just returned to the NAACP to head up a project. Brother Earl spoke often of having been mentored by W.W. Law and Ralph Mark Gilbert (1939-1956), that NAACP giant from Savanah, Georgia. I made it a habit to visit the civil rights museum there that holds much of Gibert's work whenever I go to Savannah. Earl was to me what W.W. Law had been to him.

The Clayton County NAACP was suffering from a money shortage, so Mr. Blalock and Mrs. Oukadike tried to be creative and maintain the budget by applying for county grant monies to run a summer computer class for the youths. It was Mrs. Oukadike's idea. Her daughter and Nigerian husband helped her with the program. I'm not sure how the grant money got entangled with the branch's operating fund, but it became a problem. By now we were behind in our rent and the landlord was threatening us with eviction.

One day I picked up the local paper and learned that our president and vice president were under investigation for co-mingling county's funds. I thought it was a bad idea in the first place. I went by the office and Mrs. Oukadike showed me a check which she said had a forged signature on it. She swore someone had forged her signature on the check. She was all but having a meltdown. She thought maybe she could sell the computers and pay back the $5000 the county said she stole.

The Georgia state conference president, Mr. Walter C. Butler II came to the office along with the new regional director Mr. Nelson B. Rivers III. They told Blalock and Mrs. Oukadike to step down for the sake of the reputation of the NAACP branch and seek counsel. We were evicted from the office and put the furniture in storage until we could come up with a plan. The branch had to hold a special election to elect a president and vice president to finish out the remainder of the year. I was asked to run for president, but I declined for fear that l wasn't ready for so great a responsibility. I opted for the vice president spot instead. The election was held and Mr. Bill Mouzon became president, I became his vice president, and a brilliant young lady named Frenda Norwood became secretary.

We arranged to hold our executive committee meetings in the fellowship hall at Andrews Chapel United Methodist Church at 122 Watterson Street in Jonesboro, Georgia. This church had been the birthplace of the branch in 1986. We arranged to hold our membership meetings at Dixon Grove Baptist Church at 7690 Fielder Road also in Jonesboro. That year started off bumpy. Many of the prominent members had left the branch following the county money scandal and Frenda Norwood, our secretary, would also leave soon.

Mr. Mouzon proved to be duplicitous as a president. Like me he had been with the branch for at least three years, so he understood the achievements as well as the unfinished business of the branch. But he had a questionable relationship with the chairman of the Clayton County Board of Commissioners, Crandle Bray and other commissioners, and he was trying to get a contract with the county to sell some kind of chemical. I for one didn't want any involvement with the county following the indictment of our former vice president. Besides, there was an old saying, "a dog can't bite with a bone in his mouth." If the white power structure gets our president in their hip pocket, we would have a hard time trying to make demands for justice. I felt that the president should have focused on restoring the reputation of the branch. We needed the financial support of our longstanding donors who were mainly our churches. And we needed those gifted men and women who had sustained the branch from 1986 to the present. Mouzon seemed bent on running those people away.

Mrs. Oukadike had been sentenced to serve so many days in jail. She had a severe medical condition that we feared would be aggravated if she had to do a long stint in jail. So, I went to meet with District Attorney Bob Keller, and reminded him of the white teenagers who had bombed our office and how the branch leaders were lenient about pressing charges. A deal was worked out to give the teens a hefty fine and community service. Keller agreed to let Mrs. Oukadike serve on weekends only and finish up with community service. I would constantly have to babysit Mouzon. He was short in statue, and he was always threatening to fight someone.

Mouzon attended Shiloh Baptist Church in Jonesboro with Ms. Ash, and they had some long-standing issues from there. For some reason Frenda stepped down and Ms. Ruth Ash became secretary. Ash was very strict about adhering to NAACP policy. And Mouzon didn't like that one bit. He threatened to take her outside and beat her silly on a few occasions. I had to remind him several times that he was out of order, and that he should conduct the branch's meetings according to Robert Rules of Order. Sometimes he would act professionally and carry out his basic duties, and other times he was clearly trying to serve his own agenda.

"Looka here buddy," Mouzon said so often. "I'm a Geechee, and we Geechees don't take no mess from nobody!" Deep down inside he had a heart of gold, a family man, who feared God. I would recommend certain books for him to read to help him brush up on the knowledge and mission of the NAACP, but he would brush me off. Some of the members were getting agitated at his uncouth way of running things. The year ended, and the regular election was held. and in November of 1994 I was elected president and Michael Ligon, a police detective, became my vice president. In addition to tackling the unfinished business of making Clayton County inclusive of black folks in County positions, I asked the branch members to join me in setting the branch on course to restoring it back to its own office, so we can handle our cases without meeting the complainants at the library, Waffle Houses, or residences. I asked them to help me cut out wasteful spending, engage in big fund-raising ventures, and sacrifice where they could.

We started the African American Leadership Roundtable luncheon which would be hosted at our churches, a restaurant, or another public place. At these luncheons or breakfasts, we would evaluate where we were in the county as a people. Sometimes we invited elected officials so that we could communicate our demands. We started the Family Empowerment Dinners close to Thanksgiving. We charged $20 a plate. Usually, held these dinners at North Clayton High school or North Cut Middle School. At these dinners we would invite school board members, police chiefs, commissioners, and Parent-Teacher-Student-Association presidents to give us their perspective on progress or lack thereof in their different fields. Our major fundraiser was the prestigious Freedom Fund Banquet. Sometimes our speaker would be the Hon. John Lewis, Atlanta Mayor

Bill Campbell, Georgia Attorney General Thurbert Baker, or another prominent leader. We would raise around $20,000. We gave an honorarium to our speaker, but some of them donated their time. Congressman John Lewis never took our money. If anything, he would write a check.

Ms. Ash made sure our assessments and reports were submitted to the state, regional, and national offices on time; thereby, keeping us in right standing with the association. She asserted a lot of authority. At times I would remind her of the president's role. But I must admit, much of what I learned about the NAACP came from her. She was the office manager for the Georgia State Conference of the NAACP and the Fifth Regional office of the NAACP. And like me, she was determined to keep the branch from being embarrassed again. I learned that Ruth received her B.S. degree in Elementary Education at Albany State University the year I was born. She went on to complete her M.S. degree in Elementary Education at Fort Valley State. Her knowledge about the school system was a tremendous help as we fought for the hiring and promotion of more black educators in Clayton County.

No checks were signed without a voucher from Ruth, and no voucher was issued unless the spending had been allocated by branch leaders. She ran a tight ship. Some members had some good ideas, and they would be very enthusiastic about implementing them, but Ms. Ash would remind us of the do's and don'ts of the association. I had the privilege of going into the field and executing branch decisions, knowing our secretary had our backs, and because of a strong vice president and an informed executive committee, we were able to accomplish much work in Clayton and other counties.

There were times when I would pay my own way to the state and regional conventions so we could save up our money for the office. Although I worked at the post office, I would find time to meet with an official to address discrimination cases. Once, I received three complaints from Black Clayton County Police officers. I invited Detectives Victor Hill, Gregory Porter, and Jeffrey Turner to my house to fill out their complaint forms for us to get involved. They claimed that white officers were writing "nigger" on their lockers and desk. They had been receiving racist notes, and they were being passed over for promotion. I was aware of the hiring disparities for people of color at the Clayton County Police Department, so we decided to evaluate the department inside and out. I wrote a letter to Chief Ronnie Clackum requesting his Equal Employment Opportunity Report 4 (EEO4) under the Open Records Act. This report shows the breakdown of hiring and pay by race and gender. When I received the report, it revealed that of the 232 officers in the department, only about 27 of them were Black, and of those only around two or three were above the rank of sergeant. We learned also that white leaders used a racially biased test to deny black officers a promotion. We set up a meeting with Clackum. My vice president and I went into his office to present the numbers to him, and to challenge the promotion test.

Chief Clackum put up a resistance at first, but I warned him that I was going to file a complaint with the Justice Department and call for the withholding of federal funds until he came into compliance with the law and stop discriminating against black officers; moreover, I told him that we had received complaints about White officers writing racial slurs on the lockers of black officers. Finally, I told him if these problems were not resolved quickly, we would begin holding public demonstrations in front of his police station to, in the words of Dr. King, dramatize the injustice. I held a brief press conference with Clayton News Daily, and it was on the front page the following day. In fact, we were in the local papers so much that I would see those bold letters NAACP on almost every coffee table in the various county offices we visited.

Every now and then I would write a letter to the editor railing against some injustice which would be published in the paper the following day. I wanted to stir up the county so that all elected officials knew that the black community was no longer accepting the status quo. The police chief did get rid of the racially biased promotion test, and I started seeing Jeff Turner speaking for Clayton County Police Department on TV following certain crimes. Hill and Porter received promotions also, and the department cracked down on racial slurs. There was one occasion when Clackum and I found ourselves standing face to face and toe to toe in front of Clayton County Board Chairman Crandle Bray, over Clackum's refusal to bend more on hiring and promotions. It was a very heated exchange. My vice president at the time was Mr. Willie Glen Hill (now deceased).

Glen would always recount that incident in its entirety to whoever would listen. The argument did yield some results. Many times, Mr. Willie G. Hill and I would use a "good cop, bad cop strategy" to resolve some of these discrimination cases. One of us would expose the weakness of our opponent. The "white establishment" in Clayton County was running out of time. They knew it, and we knew it. The demographics were shifting in our favor. But it was as Frederick Douglass declared so famously "Power concedes nothing without a demand." My aim was to make enough fuss so that white leaders understood that the status quo was no longer good enough, and so that black voters would know instinctively how to vote.

Many of the older blacks were used to the White politicians coming to their churches and promising them crumbs. They could either vote for one white candidate or another one, and none of them were willing to give black folks contracts, promotions, or top positions in the county. At best they would put a token black here or there. We wanted structural change. By keeping Clayton County on the evening news and in the local paper we were wearing down white voters and stimulating black voters to demand more. Some blacks saw whites as all powerful and I knew we had to attack that mindset.

One day I addressed Mayor Charles "Chuck" Hall at the Forest Park City Hall. He and Councilman Buckholt were being stubborn applying a certain city ordinance fairly. The city wanted to stop drivers from parking their privately owned eighteen-wheel trucks on their private property. But they allowed white drivers to be grandfathered in, so they didn't have to comply. The black drivers were not given grandfather status. I pointed my index finger at Mayor Hall while I scolded him and the all-white council for their reckless behavior. They were in a dilemma. I was representing two black truck drivers, Mr. Willie Finch and Mr. Shelly Barber. Both men were in their early 70s. They were used to going along to get along with white leaders. I wanted to change that and encourage them to attend council meetings and speak up when they disagreed with their elected officials.

I warned the council that the ordinance would apply to all, or it would apply to no one. After the meeting adjourned. I had a one-on-one meeting with Mayor Hall. He acknowledged the flaw and vowed to make it right. As I was leaving, Mr. Finch walked up to me and said " Man who is you? I ain't never seen a black man stand up to white folks like this!" I told Mr. Finch "That's what is wrong in our community. We let people treat us any kind of way." We went on to solve many problems in Forest Park, and we empowered the black citizens there. Another young lady who was at the council meeting that evening was Ms. Sparkle

Kornegay. I encouraged her to attend the council meeting and run for office. She did, and later became the first black person to be elected to the Forest Park city council. Today the mayor of this city is black.

I realized from traveling throughout Georgia that there were many towns and counties where it seemed black folks were stuck in time. It was as though when Dr. Martin Luther King Jr. was assassinated in 1968, the fire of the struggle almost went out. The movement came to a crawl. Some black leaders had become politicians and that was all they were. I wanted to empower the masses. I saw the disconnect, much of it had to do with education. This motivated me to become a teacher-leader. At meetings

and speaking engagements, I would do as Dr. King had done and explain the law and the history. Many of the workers we helped had no understanding of the 1964 Civil Rights Act, Title VII. They had very little knowledge of the Equal Employment Opportunity Commission and its role in safeguarding their employment rights. In fact, until I joined the NAACP and got trained, I also knew little about these things. It was Mr. Nelson B. Rivers III who taught me about requesting the EEO4 report from public agencies to evaluate their compliance with the Equal Employment Opportunity Act.

I trained others and we formed one of the most powerful labor and industry committees in the Georgia State Conference of the NAACP. Knowledge is power! I kept my reading habits up. I would read up on current NAACP events as well as the history of the organization. I recognized its shortcomings as well as its strengths. At times I felt the organization was too top heavy, and slow, but other times I was just proud to be a member. There was a saying that I came to believe, "black folks will call on two powers- Jesus Christ and the NAACP." I knew I had to protect that name and live up to the legacy black folks came to expect from us. Moreover, I was aware of the broader message that we, in Clayton County, were sending to the metro Atlanta area, and beyond. I saw other leaders standing up around Atlanta, and I like to think that the Clayton County Branch of the NAACP had some influence on them. I would certainly get calls from other civic leaders in the area to join them in protests or strategy sessions. I learned from them and shared what I had learned in my experience. I tried to avoid the temptation of competing with other civil rights leaders. The struggle for me is one.

Racial tension flared up in Riverdale, the city where I lived. It turns out that an officer had been using racial slurs on his patrol car radio. Black officers at the Riverdale Police Department were also faced with nooses behind the station. My vice president and I met with the mayor, Mary Lee and her police chief Phillips. The mayor wanted to smooth things over, and to make both incidents isolated events, but further probing revealed that it was systemic. We called for the resignation of the chief and a penalty for the officer who used racial slurs. I learned that Chief Phillips only had a 7th grade education. I thought about my own history of having dropped out of school in the 7th grade. I felt sorry for my white brother, but the times were changing. If we were going to dismantle this "good ole boy" construct we had to start somewhere. I informed the mayor that if the police chief didn't resign and the officer making the racial slurs was not punished, then her city was going to be sued and that we would begin our public demonstrations immediately. The mayor let the chief resign, and the other officer was transferred somewhere else.

We received another complaint involving the city of Riverdale. This time the complaint came from a Riverdale firefighter named Demetrius Wells. He stated that he and a white firefighter had been horse playing, and he threw the white firefighter to the ground real hard. Mr. Wells looked like he played linebacker for the Green Bay Packers. Who in his right mind would want to challenge him to a wrestling match? I wondered. The mayor and city manager, Jeff Moon were threatening him with getting a psychiatric evaluation or be terminated. He had already been written up for breaking the policy of horse playing. I listened to all three of them and then I pointed out the obvious. If the city has a no horse playing policy, then why wasn't the white employee also written up and made to get a psychiatric evaluation? Neither city leader could answer me with a straight face. I advised them that by punishing the black employee and not the white one, they were setting the city up for a labor lawsuit. Moon and the mayor agreed. I knew that racism was so entrenched in that city that I should check the Riverdale EEO4 report as we did with the Clayton County Police Department. Sure enough, when we got their EEO4 Report we saw the same disparities. All the top paying jobs were held by whites and all the blacks were in the entry level positions. There was one token black who was a Lieutenant. He was Lt. Joseph. I told the city manager and the mayor that they needed to do more to address these disparities before we filed a DOJ complaint and call for the withholding of federal funds. They complied. In fact, the city hired a black police chief, and promoted Wells.

Three cities in Clayton County (Forest Park, Morrow, and Lake City) refused to close their cities in honor of the Dr. Martin L. King, Jr. holiday. The state offices and the county seat in Jonesboro were closed, as well as the other three municipalities. We attended the city council meetings for each, Forest Park, Morrow, and Lake City to call on them to honor the holiday by closing. The leaders at the Forest Park city council told us that they gave their employees an option as to which holiday they wanted for an off day. I knew they were snubbing the holiday. I told them that if they didn't join the rest of the county and the state of Georgia in closing in honor of the holiday we were going to start protesting, and if necessary, we would call for a selective buying campaign (boycott) against Farmers Market, which was a major revenue-generating center for that city.

We held a press conference expressing our concerns. The mayor called me and told me that the city of Forest Park would close on that federal holiday. I went to Morrow, and they too dug in their heels. I threatened to boycott South Lake Mall, the county's only Mall. Mr. Steve Reick was manager of the mall at the time. He had heard about my intentions, and he must have said something to Mayor Jim Milliron, because the mayor and I found ourselves at Clayton State University attending a leadership planning session around how we could utilize all the county assets to bring more business into the county. The question was put to me, and I answered, "Clayton County cannot expect to have "New South" success, while practicing 'Old South' ways." The moderator asked me to elaborate. I looked at Mayor Milliron and said, let's take Morrow for instance. This city refuses to honor the Martin Luther King, Jr.holiday with the rest of the county and the state. Mayor Milliron interrupted and said you are wrong because the council has voted to close the city for the holiday. I said to him "This is the first I heard about it!" He said, " That's alright, It has been done." Rev. Marie and her husband Wes Greene looked at me and smiled. Both were life members of the NAACP.

I had another run in with District Attorney Bob Keller. This time he was trying to block Rev. Wes Greene, a black insurance agent, from collecting $20,000 worth of consultant fees from Clayton County after providing the service to county employees. Keller was saying that if Greene took the money, he would be double dipping in county funds since he served on the Clayton County Water Board. I happened to know that there were several white people double dipping because they served on two or more boards. And white people in Clayton County had been doing it for years.

Cronyism and nepotism had been running rampant in the county with impunity. I told Keller I wanted to convene a grand jury investigation to investigate this double dipping matter and see if this rule was being applied evenly across the board. He was reluctant at first, but then he agreed to convene one. The Greene's gave their testimony, and I identified other persons that had been serving on two or more boards and receiving payment from the county. I told them, "In fact, the doctor of the chairman of the board of commissioner, Crandle Bray was Dr. Musso, and he was awarded a two-million-dollar contract to serve the inmates at the new jail facility, and he served on the Housing Authority board. After the grand jury, Greene received his payment for his services. People who had been serving on two and three boards started resigning.

In addition to handling a variety of discrimination cases, I found time to be social. Every year Clayton County hosted a Civil War Battle re-enactment. In the month of April some in the county celebrated Confederate Memorial Day. They have a certain church service, where a local historian talks about the "lost cause." I decided to attend. I walked in the church just before the proceedings began, and I sat behind State Sen. Greg Hecht and State Rep. Frank Bailey. I placed my hands on their shoulders and greeted them. Greg, who is Jewish, turned around and said "Oh hi Rev. Wheeler. I'm surprised to see you here." He told me he came out of respect for his constituents. I told him I understood. I was there out of curiosity. Frank was equally apologetic. I reminded them that Confederate history was American history and therefore all our history.

After the church service we all assembled at the Confederate cemetery. A NAACP member was driving by as I walked with the crowd into the cemetery. The historian was also trying to be apologetic by telling his audience that there were blacks who fought on the side of the South as well. I told him later when we were alone that blacks fought under duress, and some were offered their freedom for helping the war effort, and a whole battery deserted and joined the North down in New Orleans. I told him I was a history buff. A few days later that certain NAACP member, Curtis Green said to me "Was that you I saw going into the Confederate cemetery with those white people?" I said, "That was me!" He said, "Man, you're crazy!" We both laughed. My goodness, how times were changing.

I realized something after we had convinced the city leaders to honor the MLK holiday. There was no parade for MLK Day in Clayton County. It made no sense to ask others to honor the holiday when black people weren't honoring it. That prompted me to meet with the Worshipful Master of the Elijah Summit, Mr. Herman Turner, who invited me to the lodge across the street from Andrews Chapel UM Church where the branch met. I had never been in a Masonic lodge before, let alone address its membership. But Mr. Turner gave me the floor. I explained to them that the NAACP was a bit too controversial to head up an MLK parade. We needed a neutral organization, one that was trustworthy to lead us. I told them that I would gather for them the fire engines, high school bands, law enforcement vehicles, Tuskegee Airmen, Buffalo soldiers, and others if they would be the host organization. They agreed, and we went to work.

The Clayton County MLK parade has been going steady for two decades or more. And it has surpassed the 4th of July parade in crowd size. Seeing so great a crowd of black folks in Clayton County at the first county MLK parade gave us a snapshot of the black population growth in the county. We would check the census figures every decade as we worked to register voters. We knew we had to leverage our voting power to affect the kind of change we sought.

When Vanessa, Aundria, and I first came to Clayton County to live, the black population was only 12%. Between gentrification in Atlanta in the 90s and white flight in the county the black population kept growing. Nothing made this more apparent than the local politicians' constant tinkering with the political maps. Black people were starting to compete for elected positions.

Councilman Wallace Norrington had been serving on the Jonesboro City Council since the founding of our NAACP branch. He was the only black elected official in the whole county. Then, Ms. Virginia Gray won a seat on the county's board of commissioners. We knew our political influence was shifting when Marshal Newsome was elected to the county coroner's post. This was a county-wide post. If a black person could win that seat it stands to reason that a black person could win the Sheriff seat, District Attorney, Chairman of the Board of Clayton County Commissioner, Tax Commissioner, County Clerk, etc. Frederick Douglass said, power concedes nothing without demands. He was right. The Democrat white power structure got busy with gerrymandering the maps to keep blacks away from the School Board, Commissioner seats, as well as the State Senate and House seat.

The NAACP, Rainbow Push, Southern Christian Leadership Council (SCLC), and others had been working on removing the Confederate emblem from the Georgia state flag. We met downtown at the Georgia Dome during Super Bowl XXXIV in 1994 and we marched and chanted. The Rev. Jesse Jackson, Congresswoman Maxine Waters, the Hon. State Rep. Tyrone Brooks, Joseph Boone, Rev. Orange, Dr. Joseph Lowery, Fred Taylor, Mr. Walter Butler, and many others protested at the game. Governor Roy Barnes and Lt. Gov. Mark Taylor were leading the fight to change the flag at the Georgia capitol. I had asked the Clayton County legislative delegates to stand with the black community in our quest to change the state flag. Of the seven members, five stood with us and two did not. State Rep. Ron Dodson of Forest Park opposed changing the flag, and he gave me his reason. He said his constituents wanted to preserve Georgia's heritage. Rep. Bill Lee and I had a somewhat heated argument on the phone in which he sought to remind me of my place. He and Sen. Terrell Starr were the major power brokers in the county. Sen. Starr was the third most powerful man in Georgia, and he didn't get there by being a dummy. He knew how to wield power and make deals; nevertheless, the winds of change were blowing. Starr was a life member of the NAACP. He looked out for the programs supported by Rev. Charles Grant, the African American who started the first NAACP branch back in 1955.

Grant used to ride his bike from a Black area around Hapeville called Plunket Town to gather memberships for the branch. He was very wise and scholarly. In addition to pastoring, he facilitated the start of civic leagues in the various county municipalities. He was also a businessman. He owned a day care service, where my wife once worked. But one venture that captured the essence of his service to humankind was the Clayton County Community Center at 1000 Main Street in Forest Park, Georgia. There he helped the homeless, battered women, and people who were hungry. He helped people find jobs, and he was one of my best friends. He was the one who encouraged me to run for branch president. And he advised me on many situations. He attended every Freedom Fund Banquet we had, and he wasn't afraid to write a check. Sen. Terrell Starr helped him maintain the funding for the community center. Sen. Starr and the other white delegates brought home the funding that turned Clayton State college into a university. They did remarkable work in Clayton County including expanding the interstate 675. He influenced the expansion of Hartsfield-Jackson Airport. I can look all around Clayton County and see Sen. Starr's footprint; nevertheless, we had grown weary of coming to the white Democrats with our hats in our hands, asking them to respect Black folks' interests. I knew the black population was above 50%. Why ask others to look out for our political interests when we could elect people of color to do it?

The Georgia state flag issue did more to move us in this direction. Knowing that the Confederate emblem on the flag stood for resistance to the political, economic, and social aspirations of Black folks, getting rid of it represented a pushback from the black community. In 2003, I was in Lt. Governor Mark Taylor's office representing Clayton County, when at a little after 12 midnight, the votes carried in the Georgia Assembly to remove the emblem from the state flag. I don't think any of us civil rights leaders were ready for the white backlash from Republicans and Conservative Democrats. In 2002 Gov. Roy Barnes was defeated by Sonny Perdue, the first

Republican governor elected in Georgia since Reconstruction. By 2003 former Georgia liberal Democrat governor, now US Senator Zell Miller had begun excoriating his own party in favor of the Republicans. He had given a rousing speech for Bill Clinton at the Democrat Convention in 1992, and as governor of Georgia he had fostered many liberal projects, but now the climate had clearly changed. I found myself wondering if winning the flag issue was worth it. Eventually, Republicans would go on to capture both chambers of the Georgia Assembly, and even though all seven of the Clayton County legislative delegates would become occupied by African Americans, they could do very little to advance a progressive agenda. Politics is a game of chess, and you can't take your eyes off the board, or you will miss something.

I worked with our political action committee to increase our voter registration activity at Wal Mart, Kroger, Sams Warehouse, and other places in the county. At one time Mrs. Christine Rickett chaired the political action committee, followed by Mrs. Scott. I visited black churches where pastors allowed me to address their congregations to explain the issues and do voter registration drives. At the MLK parade we would encourage participants to register and vote. Some of the municipalities had at-large voting arrangements rather than district voting so the same white voters could keep re-electing the same people to office. We fought against these arrangements. When they were changed, more blacks got elected. There were times when certain Blacks got elected who weren't compatible with the office or our interests. In fact, some of them were more corrupt than the whites they replaced. Our coroner Marshall Newsome came under investigation for swindling the government out of money through bogus Medicaid claims.

He was charging the state for transporting patients who he never picked up. He filed a complaint with us, and I was concerned that he may have been a target of some racist investigation by the Georgia Bureau of Investigation (GBI). Afterall, he was the first Black elected to a county-wide office in Clayton County. Some of us thought that Newsome might have ruffled feathers when he showed up at the Eagle's Landing Golf Pro shop riding in his limousine the night that he won the election. Surely, some whites felt he was an uppity Negro. I went over to take his complaint myself. I asked him to show me his records and prove to me that the state's case was frivolous. He refused to show me. I advised him to get a good lawyer, because there was nothing we could do. A reporter asked me to comment on the case, and I told him we had some concerns about the veracity and the timing of the investigation, but beyond that we had no further comments. Marshall Newsome was incarcerated for Medicaid fraud.

There was one executive member at our branch who stood out from the rest, a spunky, erudite sister named Valencia Seay. She said Mrs. John Dale Johnson had been one of her mentors, and it showed.

John Dale had been the director for the Atlanta NAACP branch. There is an old saying "She didn't play the radio," which meant if you saw John Dale and a bear fighting, help the bear. John Dale had resolved many civil rights cases for the NAACP in Atlanta and probably throughout Georgia. She was a beloved leader of the NAACP until she died. Valencia became our first black member of the Clayton County School Board, and in that position, she was able to get a predominantly white recalcitrant school board to name three schools for African American educators. To this day I don't know how she secured the votes to do it. I encouraged her later to run for state representative, and after her first term I pleaded with her to run for the senate seat, and let another African American take her seat. She thought I had lost my mind at first, but she listened and won, and I got Victor Hill to run for her seat and he won. Hill wanted to become Sheriff, but he had no political experience. He served in the house to terms before winning the Sheriff seat.

During a second attempt, our Democrat friends in Clayton County tried to hold on to power through gerrymandering. This involved Sen. Terrell Starr. He needed to incorporate all the older white and black voters in the 44th district that had undergone a big demographic shift. Certain Clayton County Commissioners were also threatened by this demographic shift. We understood their strategies and warned them against discriminating against black voters. They drew up the maps anyway and tried to get them passed at the Georgia Assembly. Luckily for us, State Rep. Valencia Seay was able to hold the maps in committee. We called a press conference and blasted the Democrats for gerrymandering. The next day I got a call from Sen. Terrell Starr. We met at the IHOP restaurant in Riverdale for lunch. We greeted each other and sat down. I knew why he wanted to meet with me, but I allowed him to tell me. I was tired of coming to the white power structure with my hat in my hand. And I was mindful of what Malcolm X said – "we must learn to "control the politics and the economics of our community."

Sen. Starr expressed a desire to continue in his position long enough to finish a certain amount of work that would benefit Clayton County. But I couldn't predict the end of white flight, nor could I predict the end of black migration to the county. We had to strike while the iron was hot; besides, many elections went by, and each time our hopes were dashed to the ground because our candidates lost. Black people would always be *on the outside looking in* if we didn't make a change. I told Starr the maps were racist, and we couldn't stand by and let them pass. We agreed to disagree and parted ways. Sen. Starr was admitted to Emory Hospital a very short time later. He died not long after that.

In a way that was the end of an era. Starr had done so many wonderful things for Clayton County and the state of Georgia. He didn't know just how informed I was about his work. I was also aware of the insurance contracts he had with the municipalities and our public schools. All the white mayors were well connected to him. I was appalled at the meager education level of some of them. But I saw how some of the mayors benefitted financially from their positions just like Starr. In fact, going behind the scenes of the neo-Dixiecrat machine truly enlightened me about how business was conducted. When I confronted the mayors for not honoring the MLK holiday, I saw just how vulnerable they really were, and how naive black Claytonians were, preachers included. The neo-Dixiecrats bought and sold properties, doled out contracts to their cronies, and threw a few crumbs to black folks. We were determined to bust up this operation and give more opportunities to black folks. I knew that one way to help this process was to bring media attention to bear upon these shady relationships and stir up resentment among black voters. By getting more black folks elected, we would be "At the table instead of being on the menu," as Mr. Jeffrey Benoit likes to say. The old attitudes persisted among the white power structure; the old South was still alive.

We were about to have our eleventh annual Freedom Fund Gala, and I sent a letter to Mayor Joy Day of Jonesboro to request a proclamation. She replied saying it was forthcoming. I had some business in the area, so one day I decided to stop by her office and get it. I knew she worked for the public school system by day, so I had planned to get the proclamation from the secretary. I went into the office and stopped at the receptionist's desk. There was an elderly white gentleman lying on a couch to my left. I introduced myself to the receptionist and told her why I had stopped by. She said, "The Mayor is not in at the moment, but I can take down your number, and have her call you as soon as it [document] is ready." I thanked her and turned to leave when the gentleman on the couch said, "You people need to learn to get things in on time!" I said, "Excuse me!" He started again but was interrupted by the receptionist. "Don't listen to him" she said. "I will tell the mayor you stopped by." I asked the gentleman " To whom am I speaking?" He said, "I am the mayor pro temp!" I stared into his eyes, and said, "First of all, I don't accept lectures from strangers! And second, I wasn't talking to you, but what's your name? I'll tell the mayor we had a conversation." He rose quickly from the couch and bolted out the back door. I followed him because I didn't want to give him a chance to get a weapon, or something to harm me.

He ran to his car and drove away at high speed. I went back to my office and wrote the mayor a letter about the situation. The mayor sent the proclamation letter along with an apology. She assured me that it would never happen again. I attended the next Jonesboro city council meeting to learn more about this guy. He was Councilman Shelley, and he was not the mayor pro temp. He kept fidgeting as I stared at him. I stayed for the entire meeting. I wanted to know the tenor of the meeting, whether there were any racial overtones. Councilman Norrington, the sole black member, recognized me, and acknowledged my presence. When the meeting adjoined, I shook hands with Norrington, the Mayor and other Council members, but Shelley bolted for the door. I'm sure he had been used to speaking to black folks in a condescending tone. I was not having it.

The city of Jonesboro was founded exactly 100 years before I was born. The Warren House, a two-story structure that sits on Hwy 54 near downtown is said to have been the place where the amputated legs of Confederate combatants was piled to the second story. There are a few plantation houses in the city, but the most famous is Stately Oaks. Every year they have a celebration. It was said to be the inspiration for the house Scarlett O'Hara lived in for the movie Gone with the Wind. One of the things I tried to do as President of the Clayton County branch of the NAACP was to locate as much of the footprint of the black citizens of Clayton County as possible, so that tourists coming to Clayton County would also see the black experience. We found slave graves here and there, and I learned of prominent black farmers in the area, but we were not successful in gathering enough artifacts for a museum.

I haven't given up yet. Those with power and influence tend to preserve what is meaningful to them, and of course those without money and power must work harder to preserve their heritage. I have observed this throughout the country. Clayton County has truly changed over the years. Today every member of the Clayton County Board of Commissioners is black, all the legislative delegates are Black, most of the schoolboard is Black. All the Council persons in the City of Riverdale is black, Jonesboro City Council has more people of color, so does Lovejoy, Morrow, Lake City, and Forest Park. The black population here has truly grown. Of the 298,374 people in Clayton County, African Americans make up around 72% while Whites make up around 9% in 2020. Many of the newcomers are not aware of great civil rights battles fought here. Even I cringe when I think about what life was like for black people here in the 50s 60s, and 70s. While I was stationed here in 1980-81, and from 1982-84, I was shielded by the military. But I used to hear stories from soldiers about being poorly treated by the police in these parts. I hung out in Atlanta in the West End and Greenbriar areas, or on Simpson Road.

I graduated Magna cum laude from Beulah Heights College (it was not yet a university) in 1994. I was the Valedictorian that year. In my six-minute speech, I talked about the shock that many Christians would have if Jesus returned accompanied with a multi-racial band of angels. I was reflecting on some of the resistance I received from the aging white staff when I introduced the concept of having a church service conducted by other nationalities in their language and culture. My words were received with thunderous applause and a standing ovation, but it could have been because it was only 6 minutes long, and my fellow students were ready to receive their diplomas.

I certainly was honored that day. In all fairness, those wonderful stewards of Beulah Heights did break with their old traditions and embraced the inevitable. Not only did the student body continue browning, but the faculty started browning as well. During my last year there, I met two black professors from the Interdenominational Theological Center (ITC). One such person was Prof. Rodney Jackson, the brother of Atlanta's own, Pastor Wiley Jackson. During one classroom discussion I raised a point about the civil rights engagement with the church beyond Dr. King's Letter from the Birmingham Jail. Prof. Jackson didn't shy away from the topic as some of my white professors had done previously. He elaborated on the topic and then he said "You need to go to ITC. There are volumes of books on that subject." There were other topics on the black struggle that we would discuss, and he would tell me again that I would truly benefit from studying at ITC. I was impressed and made plans to go there.

I went to the seminary to meet some of the professors and tell them about my intentions, and to learn about the history and culture of the school. I spoke with students and faculty alike, who warned me that ITC was a school of rigorous study. They said upon completion I may even question my faith in God. After witnessing the miracles in Germany and Italy, I didn't think I could encounter anyone or any teachings that would rob me of my faith in God. But I wanted to engage the sources that brought about the enlightenment of Dr. Martin L. King Jr. and other great leaders. When it came time for me to enroll at ITC I was contemplating enrolling at the John Marshall Law school, but it was facing some accreditation challenges and I entered ITC in 1995.

Dr. Calvin Morris, a man who had strategized with Dr. King, was welcoming us. He and other foot soldiers had gathered at Pascal Restaurant near the Atlanta University Center (AUC) the evening Dr. King was assassinated. He said they felt lost. They wept as they prepared for the funeral. Dr. Morris related so many beautiful stories about the movement that I could hardly wait to delve into my studies there. Dr. Morris said to the new seminarians that they were all confused when King was assassinated. They didn't know the way forward. I believe the masses of black people felt that way at the time along with a lot of anger. It seems today, we still don't know the way forward, especially when right-wing extremists are constantly strategizing to undermine any new efforts toward progress.

I had to have 90 credits to get my Master of Divinity (MDiv.) degree. So, I was careful to avoid the electives for now. I needed to take the Ethics and Society course which was related to philosophy. Dr. Riggins Earl Jr. was teaching that class. I ran into him on my way to the cafeteria. I told him that I had planned to take the course. He asked me from which school I was coming. I told him Beulah Heights. He told me that Beulah Heights students didn't do very well in his class. I too had my doubts about the preparedness of Beulah Heights students, but I was no ordinary student, I thought. I'm a book worm. And just who did he think he was slighting my school?

I assured him that I could handle the course work. He told me that he recommended that I take Introduction to Philosophy and Theology before taking a class with him. When I started taking the course with him, I understood his point. I would need to work overtime to keep up with him. He had us read Ernest Gain's Lesson Before Dying and deconstruct it using Aristotle's Nichomachean Ethics, Plato's Republic, and David Woggerman's Christian Ethics. I had never heard of Dr. Woggerman at the time, but he was the theologian that provided counsel to President Bill Clinton after the Monica Lewinsky scandal. Several of us students got together at the Woodruff Library to study and work through the assignment. Lucky for me I had already studied a little about Plato. The other books introduced me to slave narratives and the interaction between blacks and whites in the segregated South. It was a very interesting topic, and I was hungry to learn.

Dr. Earl went around the room calling on students to tell the class what they came up with. I began elaborating. Occasionally Dr. Earl would nod in approval it seemed. Finally, he said to me "That's some pretty deep shit Wheeler, but you missed the mark on that point." The class started laughing. But I knew I had a grip on the subject matter. We were given other assignments that were equally challenging. No doubt, Earl's class was my hardest up to that point and in fact he flunked half of the class. Yet, I managed to walk away with a B+.

I felt like I was among guardians of the traditions of our struggle, as well as innovators for new strategies. I had met Dr. Benjamin Elijah Mays around 1983, but now I was attending the very institution that he had helped to establish. I loved hearing the stories told by Dr. Morris about Dr. Mays. I could feel his spirit on that campus. I bought his biography, Born to Rebel and feasted on every word. It is said that Dr. Mays would push poor black students to press on despite their personal challenges. He saw something great in each student. Two of his greatest students were Dr. Martin L. King, Jr. and former Atlanta Mayor Maynard Jackson. He also taught the NAACP's one time chairman Julian Bond.

I gravitated to Mays' favorite poems, repeated so often by Dr. King: "It must be borne in mind the tragedy of life doesn't lie in not reaching your goal. The tragedy lies in having no goals to reach..." and "Whatever you do, strive to do it so well that no man living and no man dead and no man yet to be born could do it better." I tried to live by these words and teach them to others. A course in black Church History made me aware of the role of the church in our struggle. It had been our refuge in slavery, during Reconstruction, the Black Codes, Jim Crow, and the civil rights movement, all the way to the present. I learned of the denominational developments in the

Baptist traditions, Methodists (AME and UM), Presbyterian, Church of God in Christ, Lutheran, as well as the Catholic. Interdenominational Theological Center (ITC) is truly ecumenical.

Black Theology, and Liberation Theology in general really jolted me into reality. Dr. James Cone from Fordyce, Arkansas was mentioned throughout my studies at ITC. He even spoke at our annual lecture series at the chapel. I have some of his books. I did not know that the Black Power movement had impacted the American church in such a profound way. For instance, there were black caucuses formed in all the Reformed churches and the Catholic church as well to protest the racial problems of that day and the systemic racism in those institutions. I found the answer to the question I had posed to the ITC professor at Beulah Heights when I asked him if the civil rights movement had engaged the American church beyond Dr. King's Letter from the Birmingham Jail? At Beulah we merely dealt with the basic definition of theology (Theo=God, and ology=the study of). We were not taught that there was a feminist theology, a theology for the ecology, womanist theology, liberation theology, etc. Beulah had a conservative agenda that was gradually being tested.

I must admit I was leery of cold scholasticism verses the movement of the Holy Spirit. I felt that some positions in the previously mentioned theologies were not compatible with the biblical gospel of Jesus

Christ; yet, looking back at colonialism, slavery, and even today's challenges involving race, I see the relevance of these push-back theologies. Black theology addresses the shortcomings of Euro-centric theology. Today the American church and society at large are grappling with Critical Race Theory (CRT) and the 1619 Project which seeks to expose the racial underpinnings of the American experiment. They offer uncomfortable truths about the laws and historical myths that hold this nation together in its present form.

Sometimes my professors saw me on TV dealing with a civil rights issue for the NAACP. They knew I was the president of the Clayton County Branch, and they would ask me about the issues we were grappling with. Most of them were involved with or had been involved with civil rights long before I even thought about it. One of the largest cases we had to address was discrimination at the Coca Cola Company in Atlanta.

We received a complaint from Jackie James who had been fired by Coke officials for not returning to work following jury duty. James claimed that she thought she had to be on standby. Occasionally jurors are placed on standby status. She had been with the company for 14 years with no prior infractions in her personnel file. We thought this was a bit strange even in a right to work state like Georgia. We sent a letter to Coke officials requesting a meeting with their HR representative. A meeting was arranged with Mr. Jack Stahl, another white gentleman, and Ms. Ingrid Saunder Jones, a black woman who appears at major black events like the NAACP Image Awards, BET Awards, United Negro College Fund telethons etc.

Mr. Willie Scott (Clayton County NAACP Labor and Industry Chairman of the Clayton County NAACP) and Ms. Linda Rule (committee member) came with me. Scott had settled several labor cases for the branch. I sensed that by having Ms. Jones in the meeting with the two white men, Coke was trying to show us diversity and thus minimize James' complaint, but we tried to get them to see the wisdom of at least honoring their own employee handbook which gives an employee three strikes before termination. They acknowledged the rule but said James's violation was one of the company's unpardonable sins. I asked them to show me where they had terminated a White employee for committing one of these sins. They promised to get back to us with that information. This was around October of 1998.

By January of 1999 we were still waiting for the information Coke officials had promised. Between October and January time, we received several more racial discrimination complaints from Black Coke employees. Gregory A. Clark, Linda Ingrid, and Kimberly Gray Orton. We had learned that Coke was known as the "plantation" by many Black employees because promotions were very slow coming for this group. Some complained that Blacks with BA's and master's degrees were working under whites with a simple GED or high school diplomas. Some women complained that sexism prevented them from getting promotions. The number of complaints had grown so large until Scott, Rule, and I had to travel to various parts of the Metro Atlanta areas to meet with groups of them.

I sent a letter to Coke officials inquiring about the information we had requested when Ms. Jones asked for a meeting with me at the NAACP's regional office on Dr. Martin Luther King Blvd in the West End area. Mr. Nelson B. Rivers III was the regional director. He had succeeded Mr. Earl T. Shinholster. Rivers did not join us in the meeting because it was a local matter. After the small talk, Ms. Jones said to us that Coke's lawyers had advised company officials not to share the personnel information and that the company would not reinstate Ms. James. I had felt the company was going to play hardball, so we had already started preparing the other employees for a class action lawsuit against the company. But I was doing all I could to avoid this nuclear option. I said to Ms. Jones "Are you sure that Coke did not want to make Ms. James whole, and resolve some of the new complaints that we had?" She emphatically stated that Coke did not discriminate against its black employees. I said to her "You leave us no other choice." She asked, "So what will you do." I said to her "Well, you know we are a protest organization, so we will lead an active protest campaign against Coke, and if it leads to a lawsuit, we will follow that path." I do not like to bluff.

I try to always make promises.

I believed since our Regional Director, Mr. Nelson B. Rivers III, was on Coke's board, he would be their assurance that our protest would be minimal. So, we prepared the complainants to be ready to settle their issues with the lawyer Attorney Cyrus Mehri in the event the National Office pulled the rug out from under us. In the meantime, we organized press conferences to lay out our complaint before the public. We had credible speakers, some of whom had achieved high levels in the Coke structure. Few local black civil rights leaders were willing to speak against the company. Mr. Joe Beasley, Jesse Jackson's representative for Rainbow PUSH, spoke out fearlessly. And I spoke on several occasions until I got a call from Mr. Rivers, who had been transferred to the National Office, saying I was not to mention a selective buying campaign against Coke in the name of the NAACP. He was too late. I had done just that a couple of days prior.

Rivers threatened to censure me and stop me from speaking in the name of the NAACP. My attitude toward the NAACP shifted. I felt like the organization was in the hands of corporate America, and not the freedom fighters I had come to love so much. All the great things I had read about the NAACP and the work of past and present leaders were being weighed in the balance. It was Mr. Rivers who would lead us in a call and response chant at the conventions, "Fired Up! Fired Up! Ready to go! Anywhere! Anyhow! Right here! Right now!" But now it seems that he and the NAACP board members were kowtowing to Coke. Let me say here that my respect for Mr. Rivers, his leadership, and major contribution to the NAACP never waned. I recognized him early on as a very knowledgeable and dedicated leader in the Association. I learned so much from him. He had a role to play, and he played it well, all things considered. The zeitgeist has a way of using people willingly, or unwillingly.

I understood the NAACP Board members' position even though I disagreed with them. Coke had been a great friend financially. The NAACP was in the red leading up to the resignation of Dr. Ben Chavis, who served 16 months beginning in 1993. He had been forced to resign amid allegations that he used NAACP funds to settle out of court a sexual harassment lawsuit. Mr. Earl T. Shinholster was appointed Acting CEO in his stead. Earl was a steady hand at the helm. We were very proud of the work that he did. He restored the integrity as well as the financial viability of the organization. The Coca Cola Company gave 20 million dollars to the NAACP during this time. No one at the national office communicated to me why the NAACP wouldn't back the lawsuit. I was simply told that the NAACP did not have a lawsuit against Coke. I remember thinking to myself, how could the NAACP file a class action lawsuit against the soft drink giant after all of the generosity Coke gave to the organization over the years? The National Office could not sign off on this lawsuit. But I had been trained to go after injustice wherever I found it. Of course, we did our investigation to make sure the complaint was legit.

As these complaints came in, I saw the consistencies in each testimony. And I saw that Coke officials were not being forthcoming with the facts. Coke had an elaborate scheme, not unlike other corporate entities, where they make handsome contributions to black causes, and befriend prominent black leaders, while structural racism within is neatly tucked away. I noticed early on the naivete of other local civil rights leaders. We tried to meet with some to show them our findings, but they refused to even meet with us. Others met with us but refused to take a position against the soft drink giant. In the May 18, 1999, issue of the Wall Street Journal, staff reporter Nikhil Deougun wrote an article entitled, A Race-Bias Suit Tests Coke: Can the real thing do the right thing. The article talks about Coke's long-standing relationship with black political leaders specifically, and the black community in general.

Rev. Timothy McDonald, president of the Atlanta based Concerned Black Clergy, was quoted saying " If there's any good corporate citizen in terms of involvement and hiring, it's Coke." He went on to say "I don't think they'll [the plaintiffs] get a lot of support." Thomas Dortch, president of Atlanta based 100 Black Men said, "A lot of companies make billions of dollars and don't invest in the community, but Coke does, so I'm a little more sympathetic and tolerant."

He went on to say that "If Coke were ever found guilty of a pattern of discrimination, we would be aggressive in our response. But because Coca Cola has been a friend, we owe it to them to work it out, and deal with it." The article points out that Dortch had been a top aide to former US Senator Sam Nunn for a number of years, and Nunn not only sat on the board at Coke, he was also a partner with Coke's law firm King & Spalding.

Other civil rights leaders voiced their opinion about the lawsuit after it had been settled. In the June 15, 2000, issue of the Atlanta Journal-Constitution entitled Civil rights leaders differ on effect pact has on workers, community; Russell Grantham had interviewed certain of these leaders. The Hon. Hosea Williams (74) expressed worries that the lawsuit would benefit a handful of plaintiffs but do nothing to change the culture of the Coca Cola Company. He was quoted as saying "I just have mixed emotions." He said "You aren't supposed to be striking for money. You're supposed to be striking to better the pay and conditions of all of the employees." Well, this is exactly what the lawsuit did.

Dr. Joseph Lowery, former head of SCLC, seemed a bit more sympathetic to our work. He said, "I want to congratulate both the company and the employees. I think it's good for the employees and good for the company and good for the community to be settled." Lowery believed the settlement could send a message to other companies, which was what I was hoping to do. I knew that this same culture at Coke existed in most, if not all, of the major corporations. But we would never change it if our civil rights organizations and political leaders were bought and paid for. I decided not to be that kind of a leader.

During the height of the Coke battle, I received a call from Ambassador, and former Atlanta Mayor Andrew Young's office. His secretary left a message on my voice mail saying he would like to meet with me. I knew instinctively that Coke officials were going to use Young to get me to break with the complainants and align our branch with the National office of the NAACP. I called the secretary back who informed me that Mr. Young was in Africa on business, but he had asked Atlanta Life Insurance giant Mr. Jessie Hill to meet with me on his behalf, so Mr. Hill and I agreed to meet at Carrabba's Italian Bar and Grill on Mt. Zion Blvd in Morrow, Georgia for dinner. He and his lovely wife arrived, and we sat down to dine. He asked me some questions about myself like what kind of car did I drive, and what kind of house I lived in, and then he got down to business. He asked me what could be done to make this lawsuit go away? I informed him that both my house and car was paid for, and that I had no need of anything, but justice; moreover, I told him that the lawsuit was out of my hands, and that we had given Coke officials ample space to resolve this matter long before it came to a lawsuit. I thanked him for dinner and bid the couple good evening. Mr. Hill wasn't thoroughly convinced that my mind was made up because he said, " I will be in touch!"

I had read about how Dr. Martin L. King, Jr. died a lonely man. Many of the other civil rights leaders left him when he began speaking out against the Vietnam war. Yes, politics is the art of compromise, but there are some principles one must stand on. Many small indications kept pointing to deeper flaws in the company. There were several awkward moments during the battle. In addition to Coke officials shredding documents, we saw top officials shuffling leaders left and right.

At one point Chairman and Chief Executive M. Douglas Ivester sought to do damage control by putting together a Diversity Advisory Council which consisted of Carl Ware, an African American who had been senior vice president in charge of the African Group, Ingrid Saunder Jones along with Jack Stahl, senior vice president of the North America Group. The plaintiffs' lawyers saw through this window dressing and called them out. Mr. Ware, former Atlanta City Council president and 25-year veteran with Coke, spoke very highly about Coke's outstanding record on diversity in hiring and promotions, until he got the word that he was being demoted. Soon he too became part of a litigation filed against the company. Before long Ivester himself was removed from his position. Apparently, the shareholders had lost faith in him. Several blunders exposed the company's underbelly. A drop in Coke's stock didn't help either.

I tried to keep the complainants from knowing the position of the National Office. I did not want to embarrass the Association or weaken our case. So, I continued to show up at the rallies and press conferences as more complainants were added to the pool. More and more I stood back and let the lawyers conduct the meetings. We had learned through inside employees that Coke officials were shredding documents. Judge Richard W. Story had to issue the company a cease-and-desist order. There were statistical data showing that the median salary for African American employees was one third less than that of Whites. For example, at the HQ office in 1995 African Americans were paid over $19,000 less than their White counterparts, and in 1998 blacks made $27,000 less than Whites. Employees had to contend with a "glass ceiling," and a "glass wall" which blocked upward mobility and lateral moves.

Racially disparate impact is a violation of Title VII of the 1964 Civil Rights Act. These were the findings that would not allow us to lose steam regardless of all the opposition. There was one time I felt like a pariah with the NAACP. I attended the regional NAACP Convention in Greensboro, NC feeling down because the top leaders did not want to acknowledge the lawsuit, and I ran into Mr. Earl Shinholster. He fixed his eyes on me and started walking directly toward me. He stood in front of me and gave me a stern look as he took his index finger and poked me in the chess saying, "I know what you are going through, but don't you stand down!" I gave him a soul handshake and hugged him. I needed that affirmation, that reassurance that what I was doing was right. This bolstered my confidence.

I had a meeting with Atty. Cyrus Mehri and the Rev. Jesse Jackson around 3 a.m. at the Sheraton Hotel, downtown Atlanta. We were discussing plans to cause a ruckus at the upcoming Coca Cola shareholders meeting in Delaware. This protest rally would bring about the necessary pressure to get Coke to settle. I had a side bar conversation with Attorney Mehri that morning. He said to me "You are the only civil rights leader that stood with us all the way." He seemed to promise me that he would compensate me for all of my hard work once the case was settled. I expressed my gratitude for the gesture as well as his willingness to take the case in the first place. I told him that if he wanted to donate to our branch that would be fine, but I personally would not accept any money for my work. I feared that my critics would say I was in it for the money all along. But for me it was the principles.

I felt the pain of these black employees. The truth is, there are many companies that pay black people far less than whites, and they go unchallenged. Coke settled out of court with the complainants to the tune of 192.5 million dollars. It was the largest discrimination lawsuit against any company. Coke had enough influence to do damage control and minimized the information about the lawsuit. But luckily today, one can Google it. I was appalled that only three people from the Atlanta complaints came back to say thank you in a tangible way. One member donated to the branch, and two more even joined. One became a life member of the NAACP. While many of the branch members felt slighted, I pointed to the reimbursement by the lawyers for all the man and woman hours that went into solving the case.

Some of the black politicians who got elected during the late 90s turned out to be ill prepared for the offices they held, in my opinion. We would watch the Clayton County School board members on the evening news going after each other in heated exchanges. And even though blacks made up a sizeable portion of the board by then, they couldn't seem to agree on much. Mr. John Trotter, who had long left the NAACP to start his own teachers' union called Metro Association of Classroom Educators (MACE), had been instrumental in getting three Black female school board members elected - Nedra Ware, Linda Crummy, and Connie Kitchens. They tended to vote together on certain matters that sometimes even went against our interests as well as those of the majority of African American parents.

We called a meeting with the 3 ladies at Greater Solid Rock church in Riverdale, under the leadership of Dr. John Waters. Other prominent clergy persons were in attendance as well. My concern was that the ladies ignored the history of the black struggle that got us to that point in Clayton County, only to make the school board meetings look like a circus on the daily evening news. They seemed to brush off these concerns and they dug in their heels to hear John Totter's agenda. Some in the community had rumored that Trotter wanted to be school superintendent, which none of us branch members wanted. We had clamored for a superintendent of color and the board voted for an African American named Joe Hairston of Maryland. Even though Hairston leaned more toward Republicans in his politics, he was able to increase our children's test scores, and even offered up some ideas that were adopted by the state of Georgia.

Some of us branch members met with Hairston to get him to address the disparities concerning the black teacher/principal ratio to black students. We asked him to make the changes through attrition, which meant add black staff as white teachers retired or quit. We did not want white staff persons to scream reverse discrimination. Hairston made some improvements, but it didn't go over well with the white school board members. Chairman Mark Armstrong and other white board members came together and plotted to terminate Hairston's contract. The NAACP protested the decision and led a rally against them, and they backed down. The black population was steadily increasing, and each election reflected that reality. Eventually Hairston decided to accept a buyout of his contract and return to Maryland. We knew it was due to pressure.

Dan Caldwell, a Caucasian, was seated as interim superintendent. He wanted the position, but he was under a cloud of suspicion for past votes, and his good old boy status with the old guard. We also had problems with a certain firing of a black principal, Dr. Gloria Duncan. Duncan had come to the NAACP for help to get her job back. Some of the infractions the board accused her of seemed frivolous to us especially in light of the many infractions by whites who were still employed. We took up the case with Caldwell. He would not bulge on her reinstatement. Months went by, and Caldwell needed some leverage to gain support from the black community leaders. Gloria saw an opportunity to curry favor with him, so she sought to bring him to our African American Leadership Roundtable meeting and bestow some kind of honor upon him. She knew I had to work and would not be in attendance. But when I got wind of it, I drafted up a letter about Caldwell to be read in my absence at the meeting.

The letter was delivered by my VP Mr. Terry Bizzell. In a way it was a scathing letter about his reversal on progress set by Hairston, and his role in the scheme to unseat Hairston. I expressed my support for Duncan, but not the method she chose to get reinstated. Duncan later became part of a faction that sought to validate Caldwell. She was rewarded for her efforts and reinstated. There were several things I loved about Duncan. She had worked hard to earn her degrees, she was a very skillful administrator, and a dedicated educator. She belonged in the role of leading a high school. I was glad when she became the principal of Riverdale High School. I had walked through North Clayton High school one day, and I saw graffiti on the bathroom wall. I encountered young black men who were unruly, but I didn't see that at Riverdale High. Principal Duncan took me on a tour, and I watched the young men remove their head gear as we passed by. I asked her about graffiti I had seen at other schools. She looked at me and said "We don't do graffiti here! We believe in discipline." It was so refreshing to hear that, especially now that Riverdale High was around 60% black.

I mentioned Marshall Newsome's fall from grace, but another high profile African American in our county kept making the news as well – the illustrious Sheriff Victor Hill. His first bad move came when he started shuffling his deputies around, bringing his staff in line with his vision. It seems he demoted certain white employees and advanced certain black employees. It led to a reverse discrimination lawsuit in which the white employees won. I had gone to Hill's office to have a very confidential meeting with him to ask him to go slow and make changes through attrition like we had asked his former boss Chief Clackum to do, but he said something to me that suggested he had a whole different view about leadership. He asked me, "If a leader had a choice of whether he would be feared or respected, which one should he choose?" I said both, because if the leader administers policies in a fair and equitable way and uses his/her authority to enforce the rules he/she would be feared and respected.

Hill told me the leader should choose fear. He said a sheep cannot lead a pack of lions, but a lion can lead a pack of sheep. Hill was sued a second time for the same offense and his opponents won again. Some of us were starting to worry about the millions of dollars he was costing the county with these lawsuits. He lost an election amid these scandals. But he made a comeback in a subsequent election. I was hoping that he learned his lesson. He was a fine Sheriff in terms of fighting crime in the county. Not long after he came back into power, he was on the evening news again for discharging a weapon in a woman's home. The bullet struck the woman causing non-life-threatening injuries, but Hill called 911 and left the scene of the accident. The next morning, I was listening to J. Anthony Brown on the Tom Joyner radio show making all kinds of wise cracks about our Sheriff. They were saying he had a Napoleon complex, among other things. He managed to wiggle out of that scandal. But in 2021 he was indicted for violating an inmate's constitutional rights by ordering officers to strap the white inmate in a restraint chair. The inmate claims Hill left him there for hours.

Georgia's Governor Brian Kemp convened a three-person panel and had Hill suspended. A large segment of the population disagreed with the governor, and I was one of them. In my opinion, Gov. Kemp is an illegal governor. Millions of Georgians believe he stole the election from Stacey Abrams; moreover, he comes across as a Jim Crow governor to me. He removed a black mayor in 2021 over alleged malfeasance, and he constantly engages in a war of words with black Atlanta Mayor Keisha Lance Bottoms. I have yet to see Gov. Kemp take harsh actions against white elected officials, and there are plenty from which to choose. The removal of Victor

Hill was, in my opinion, "plantation" politics. And yet, I know that Hill brought some of it to himself. Gov. Sonny Perdue was called on to intervene in the Clayton County School Board fiasco in the late 90s but refused to do so. Instead, he let the School Advisory Council (SAC) threaten the board with taking away the school's accreditation if they didn't find a way to work together for the good of the students. I had hoped that all the newly elected black officials would have respect for the long struggle that it took for black folks to arrive at this juncture. One of the things I impressed upon all these leaders was to read Taylor Branch's book, Parting the Waters, and David Garrow's Bearing the Cross. Authors like these helped me to stay grounded and be very intentional about every political move I made. There were times I encountered people who I knew were trying to use my status for their own political aims, and not that of the people. Greed and corruption do not belong to one race.

At the end of the Coca Cola lawsuit, I was exhausted. We had been solving so many complaints for 8 years straight. I was meeting myself coming and going, so to speak. I had little time for family or any leisure activity. I decided and announced to the branch membership that I would not seek a fifth term in the upcoming election. Many expressed resentments especially among the clergy. Others weren't so sure they wanted me to stay or leave. At times we would have sharp disagreements over certain matters. And then there was the petty jealousy from within and without. By 2002 we had restored the branch back to the pre-Blalock era. Our financial house was on sound footing. The branch had an office on Main Street in Forest Park, Georgia. We later moved into a suite owned by Mr. and Mrs. Osborne at 20 McDonough Street right next to the old Courthouse in Downtown Jonesboro.

The Osbornes were a white couple. Harold Osborne was a banker, Karol was an active life member of the NAACP, and one of my staunch supporters. There were not many black businesses in downtown Jonesboro. I dare say it remained de facto segregated until the mid-90s.This is the county seat. The relics of the old segregation order were everywhere. Confederate flags still adorned certain landscapes. Antebellum paintings, and pictures of segregationists still hung on the walls of certain law offices and other businesses. I remember thinking to myself at our new office, Herman Talmadge would have turned over in his grave by now.

I felt like the branch and its leaders were in a good place now. If I was going to leave, now would be a good time. I assured my branch family that I would be active with them, but only in the background. I did not want to hold an office. Once I felt the need to come back as VP to assist my successor Mr. Dexter Matthew. I ran for the VP spot and won. Nevertheless, I was determined to let him hold the reins and enjoy the full weight of the office. After I retired from the Post Office in 2015, I became VP for the National Action Network (NAN) of Henry and Clayton County. I worked with NAN president Jeffrey Benoir.

Progress for the black community in Clayton County accelerated during the early 2000s in terms of getting more black people elected, and many of the architects were elected to office. I have already mentioned Valencia Seay, but another outstanding member of the executive committee was Gail Hambrick. She went on to become county commissioner. Wade Starr, a founding member and the first VP of our branch assumed a powerful county position in housing and other agencies. The celebrated former Atlanta Police Chief Eldrin Bell saw the winds of change blowing so he relocated to Clayton County following the sizeable migration of Atlanta citizens.

Bell began attending NAACP branch meetings in the late 90s. The city of Atlanta rejected his bid to become Mayor there, but he found fertile political ground in Clayton, and in 2004 he was elected the first black Chairman of the Clayton County Board of Commissioners. He also made Jeffery Turner the first black Police Chief of the Clayton County Police Department. Greg Porter became Assistant Chief. A number of Black judges were elected, such as Wanda Dallas, Geronda V. Carter, Robert Mack (NAACP), Shana Rooks (NAACP), Aaron B. Mason, Jewel Scott (NAACP), Bobby Simmons (former VP of Clayton County NAACP) and others who were affiliated with the Clayton County NAACP.

Greg Porter became the second black Police Chief of Clayton County, and Jeffrey Turner became the second black Chairman of the Clayton County Board of Commissioners. Terry Baskin (NAACP) became Clayton County Tax Commissioner. There have been several black Clayton County School Board members past and present. Mrs. Bulloch, wife of our treasurer Tony Bulloch, assumed the top position at the Clayton County Vehicle Registration office. We labored to get schools and buildings named in honor of African Americans who had made great sacrifices in our county such as M.D. Roberts Elementary School, who was a respected citizen of Clayton because he was a family man and strongly committed to education, during and after his tenure with Clayton County Public Schools, James Jackson (named for the founding president of the Clayton County NAACP), and Eddie White Academy named for one of the most powerful members of the executive committee. The erudite Mr. White insisted on following protocol in the NAACP and everywhere else he worked. He taught school in Clayton County all the way back to the segregation period of the 1960s. I drew much from his wisdom and experience.

Unfortunately, there were opportunists who sought to springboard off the branch's reputation into a lucrative elected office or a job in the county. We tried to appropriate their skills and time by getting them to serve on committees to monitor school board meetings, board of commissioner meetings, as well as the six municipalities' council meetings. The NAACP branch is a very good training ground for leadership development. But it often does nothing to reform a grifter. First Lady Michelle Obama was right when she said, "Being President, doesn't change who you are, it reveals who you are." I think this is true for any position of authority. I have watched people get elected and abuse their authority. I saw them get into positions and snub the people who helped them get elected. And some of these same people came back to the Clayton County NAACP when they came under investigation for malfeasance. They felt that they could play the race card to get out of the jam. I have witnessed several great black men and women, locally and on national levels, fall from grace because of flaws in their own character. I warned black leaders in Clayton County to be mindful of the temptation of elected office and to operate with integrity. Some listened, and some did not. There were times I found myself questioning our efforts to get so many black folks elected at one time. I would approach them about a concern, and they treated me as if I had offended them. The white elected officials that preceded them had to at least try to appease me, but some of the black elected officials felt that they were in charge now, and they would govern as they saw fit.

I received a call from Greg Porter, the newly ousted Clayton County Police Chief saying that he had been wronged by the Board Chairman. Greg along with

Sheriff Victor Hill and Clayton County Board of Commissioners Chairman Jeffrey Turner were the same three officers who sat at my kitchen table explaining their discrimination cases to me in 1994, but now in 2015 Turner wanted to get rid of Porter not over some infraction, but because of personal differences. I received a call from Captain Andre Jackson (another officer we helped) asking me not to intervene in the matter. He told me that other officers did not want to work under Porter. I told him I would get back to him. A few days later I received a call from Sheriff Victor Hill, who wanted to have lunch with me and discuss Porter's firing.

I figured Hill aspired to consolidate the Sheriff and the Clayton County Police departments, with which I totally disagreed. If Hill was seemingly intoxicated with running the Sheriff department, how much more would he be if had run both law enforcement agencies? We sat down to talk, and I listened. I expressed to him my deep disappointment over the division between the three leaders who came up in the ranks to hold the top positions in the county. Greg had told me that he was asked to go along with something unethical which he refused to do, and some of the officers became disgruntled because he held them all accountable.

Captain Jackson later was caught in a sting operation and indicted by a federal grand jury over bank fraud which proved Porter's point about having poor officer accountability. The National Action

Network contested Porter's firing. We met with Turner, Commissioner Rooks, and others to express our opposition. We later held public demonstrations at Rooks' law office, Commissioner Edmondson's office, and in front of the Clayton County Police Department. Turner and Hill sent deputies and Clayton County Police Department officers to arrest me. I extended my hands to them to be handcuffed, and told them to tell their bosses, "It is 4:00 p.m. and we are not leaving until 6:00 p.m. If you want to take me to jail, then here I am!" The officers backed down. I had planned to sue the county if I was arrested. Porter filed his own lawsuit and waited them out. I recall thinking to myself; it was easier dealing with the white leaders. We must hold all elected officials accountable regardless of race or party affiliation, if we are to have responsible government. That's a principle I stand on. .

A street connected to I-75 in the Forest Park region is named for Rev. Charles W. Grant, the founder of the first Clayton County branch of the NAACP in the 50s, which fizzled out. I used to call him my civil rights father because he was the one who pushed me to run for president of the newer chapter, and he backed me to the hilt through many civil rights battles. We used to hold political forums and African American Leadership Roundtable luncheons at his facility, the Clayton County Community Service Center at 1000 Main Street in Forest Park, Georgia. Rev. Grant enjoyed the popularity of black and white citizens of Clayton County and around the state. His eloquence had graced our local papers as well as pulpits throughout the county. His humor could disarm you, only to set you up for the theological or historical perspectives that he unleashed.

Grant had a genuine concern for the homeless, battered women, and needy children. I was so proud to call him a friend. The erudite Dr. John Waters, pastor of the Greater Solid Rock Baptist Church, and Dr. Emanuel McCall, pastor of the Christian Fellowship Southern Baptist church, would invite me to speak at the Watch Night service, and the Sunday before the MLK Holiday respectively. On these days they would always give me a check for the branch.

The pillars of the black community in Clayton County and the sustainers of our branch were Rev. Arthur Powell of Travelers Rest Baptist Church, Rev. James Harris of Dixon Grove BC, Rev. Homer Pittman, of New Pleasant Grove BC, Rev. Hopie Strictland of Mt. Olive Baptist BC in Henry County, Rev. W.C. Smith of Shiloh BC, Rev. Gerry T. Anderson of New Macedonia BC (my home church), Rev. Howard Crecy of Mount Olive BC, Dr. Cornelius Henderson of Cascade United Methodist, Rev. Wesley Green and Dr. Marie Green, and a host of other clergy men and women. I could always count on these churches to buy a ten-member table at our annual Freedom Fund Banquet, or any other fundraising efforts by the branch. I visited these churches frequently and gave them updates on the progress of black people in the county as well as the challenges.

Much of our membership came from these churches also.

Working with civic minded people to bring needed changes is infectious. I realize that I would never be able to get civil rights work out of my system, nor could I return to just being a regular citizen again. I am currently involved with the National Action Network. The fact of the matter is, there is so much work to do that must be done lest we lose the ground we gained. It is disturbing to me when I turn on my TV and hear about the rampant gun violence among our youths here in the metro Atlanta area and around the country, or when I see black elected officials shucking their responsibilities and being involved in scandals. Too many people have labored and sacrificed their all to give them opportunities to serve. The 2020 census for State of Georgia revealed that white Georgians are just over 51% of the population, followed by African Americans (31%), and Latin Americans (23%), and Asians (5%). This means more responsibilities and opportunities for people of color.

We cannot afford to squander these opportunities. There are forces in this country who are troubled by these numbers, and they are willing to employ all kinds of schemes to maintain domination. A lack of access to healthcare, disease, gun violence, high incarceration rates, voter suppression, economic suppression, and poor education are all conspiring together to slow down our advancement. We must use every tool at our disposal to wake up the masses and make them cognizant of our current challenges. We do not control most mediums that funnel information to us, and some of our young music artists are restricted to the lyrical content they can write about in their songs; likewise, many of the movies released by blacks are repetitious, and some of them are even degrading. But I believe in the transforming power of the arts. Film directors as well as certain rappers can shift the whole atmosphere. This is why I wanted to get back into music. It allows me to express some of my deepest feelings.

The new time I now had allowed me the opportunity to go into the studio and record 5 songs I had written. After failing to gain traction at Divine Faith pastor Donald Battle's studio, I found a good friend named Greg Hicks, who had just opened Sleeping Giant studio in the basement of his house in Lithonia, Georgia. Hicks was still learning to produce records, but he was very excited to work with me. He knew some great musicians and gifted background singers. I played piano at my church on Sundays. I had also been working on a reggae tune called One Step, some R & B styled gospel tunes, It's All About Christ, I'm Gonna Praise Him, and Sweet Hour of Prayer. Greg introduced me to wonderful musicians like M.J. Bell on keyboard, Greg Lockett and Donnie Rogers on bass, Anthony Van Johnson on drums, Keith Cooper on lead/rhythm guitar, and Solomon Edmond on synthesizer/keyboard. Quida McMullen, Felisha Price, and Eric Moore sang in the background.

It was a wonderful recording experience even though Greg hadn't mastered his equipment yet. We were all excited about the finished product. I recorded You Will Get Through This at 2201 Studio in College Park, Georgia. The 5-song project was mastered at In God I Trust studio in Stone Mountain, Georgia. I did my first performance at Greg's church Green Forest. When I saw Pastor Gumby get up and dance to my reggae song One Step, I knew I was onto something. That spring, I was invited to the Sweet Auburn Festival in downtown Atlanta. My music was received well there. We sold hundreds of CDs.

Soon I met Melvin Pierce, a jazz trumpeter of Snellville, Georgia and a powerful acoustic guitar/keyboardist named Christopher Lewis. I met Chris at the C-Room in Forest Park, Georgia. I sang One Step and Sweet Hour. It was received well by the audience. Chris invited me to check out Melvin's studio. Soon he and I collaborated on 4 more new tunes Praise Him with All I Have, Let's Make Music, Gotta Be Strong, and Shine from Heaven. We combined these with other songs and called the CD All to Jesus. We registered that CD with CD Baby's website, and we sold hundreds of hard copies and some downloads and streams. I was toying around with a tune in my head I called Imagine Heaven.

One morning as I was driving to the Peachtree City Post Office where I worked, I heard on the news that many people had been killed in Chicago gun violence. The lyrics for my reggae song Love's Calling began to flow through my mind. Thirty minutes later as I pulled into the parking lot I had written the complete song. I couldn't wait to get to Melvin's and put it on wax. Many of the lyrics for my songs came to me as I delivered the mail so I started carrying a digital recorder with me. I would write lyrics on any piece of paper I could find including business cards in my wallet.

One Saturday morning I arrived at my first residential stop, and the words, She sang off key in the choir, never learned to read very well, but every week she was at Bible study. She loved the Lord you could tell, came out of nowhere. About halfway through my route I finished the song, It's Not What You Say, It's What You Do. I completed two whole CD projects and other songs with Melvin at Aventra Enterprise. I met wonderful musicians who are all mentioned on my CDs. In 2014 we won the Gospel Choice Award for best male vocal. Even though it is a local award here in Atlanta, I was encouraged that my work was respected by my peers and others in the business.

I started KINTUPS Records, and Pillowhill Publishing, because I didn't want to sell my soul to the industry. I wish to be an artist on my terms. And I am grateful to God for the journey.

Singing for me is a celebration everywhere I go, big venues or small. The highlight of my music journey is when the band and I traveled to Helena, Arkansas to perform. Words cannot express what it felt like being at the pavilion where so many blues greats have performed. The Canton Spirituals performed that day after us. The money and the fans left a lasting impact on us. The first time I sang there I did so using music tracks, but having the band there was a liberating feeling. I got to see childhood friends. On Friday before Saturday's concert, the band members and I feasted on seafood at the Isle of Capri Casino buffet. We stayed at hotels in town. Some of them got a chance to meet my Aunt Vannie and other family members, as well as see historical landmarks. I had arrived at the place I had dreamed about as a child; except I was seasoned and void of the lust for attention from the girls. I wanted to sing songs that would uplift the human spirit and encourage someone to reach for higher ground. I was aware of how devastating crack cocaine had been to my hometown. My audience was all too familiar with friends and loved ones who had suffered death, imprisonment, or wrecked lives due to crack or alcohol. I wanted my message to be clear in my words and songs. My band members knew what I stood for, so we presented a united front.

Conclusion

Because racism in America is so pervasive and has been for so long, it appears to be an insurmountable challenge especially for a little NAACP organization. We NAACP members pride ourselves on being the oldest and the baddest civil rights organization around, and much of that is true. The NAACP was founded in 1909, long before the other major civil rights organizations. It even predates the United Negro Improvement Association (UNIA). The latter's founder, Marcus Garvey, may have been inspired by the NAACP. Both groups have done remarkable work nationally and locally and the NAACP is still going strong. It is said that the ANC of South Africa patterned its constitution after the NAACP, the difference between the two is that the ANC had a military wing. But racism is entrenched in the political parties, the courts, corporations, and every aspect of American life.

The civil rights organizations can't raise enough money to eradicate it. I concluded it would have to take the Almighty Himself to straighten this mess out. And even when we get the racial mess untangled, we will have to deal with the sins of our own race. Perhaps this is why Brother Malcolm and Brother Earl began talking more about human rights before they were taken from us. While most black Americans would rather take it easy and enjoy the short time we have on earth, history doesn't afford us that luxury. We must stay engaged and look for new ways to bring about our total liberation, and full inclusion into a land for which we have sacrificed so much. Moreover, we must guard against being used by the corporate elites to exploit Africa, and other lesser developed parts of the world.

This is a tall order since we have been used historically against others. We joined with others to oppose apartheid in South Africa, and we rallied with anti-colonial forces during the 60s and 70s. But the US has assassinated African leaders, Asian leaders, as well as leaders in the Middle East. The CIA and FBI have intermeddled with the affairs of South American countries, Cuba, and Haiti. It is a tricky proposition since these are ongoing operations. But we are called on to be good world citizens even as we wage our own struggle.

This is where I find myself today. As a father, grandfather, and great grandfather, I have labored to educate my daughter and grandchildren to equip them to do their part in upcoming struggles. I have more years behind me than I have in front of me, but it is my hope that I have done some good to inspire, enlighten, and encourage others to be engaged. I will continue to work with other activists until I have no more strength left. I am encouraged by the work and energy of the trailing generations. I get the chance sometimes to labor alongside them. I don't want to disturb their passion. Yet, when I see an opportunity, I share some of my experiences, and even help them plan strategies to achieve their goals. My faith in God, and my walk with Jesus the Christ, have been the strength of my journey.

I regret the fact that at times we, in the black community, have not always represented Christ well, and in the white community Jesus has been appropriated by some to propagate white supremacy; thereby, turning off so many young people of all racial background and nationalities. Still, I find no fault in the Christ of the book. I have heard some of my brothers and sisters from the LGBTQ community denounce the church and Christianity for being oppressive to them. But I feel that in my natural state, I am prone to walk in error and fulfill the lust of my flesh; nonetheless, in Christ I can see how elementary those lusts are. From them I get a temporary feeling of bliss only for the desire to be kindled again. But with Christ, my thirst for righteousness is satisfied all day long. Christ summons everyone to live in harmony, one with another. The Lord seeks not to condemn a soul, but to redeem it. I have never hated my opponents, even when I could clearly see their mischief. But like God, we must oppose evil and show forth God's righteousness. If for that reason we are despised, then we are in good company, for they despised Jesus also.

www.ingramcontent.com/pod-product-compliance
Lightning Source LLC
Chambersburg PA
CBHW061141120626
46546CB00005B/1877